MINNESOTA TERRITORY

WISCONSIN

MICHIGAN

Mississippi River

Missouri River

IOWA

ILLINOIS

Council Bluffs

Nauvoo

Fort Leavenworth
Independence

MISSOURI

NEW YORK

N.H.

MASS.
CONN.
R.I.

Mormon Trails

—— Mormon Trail

Mississippi Saints

········· Continental Divide

········· Mormon Battalion

○ Points of Interest

ARKANSAS

GEORGIA

ALABAMA

MISS.

LOUISIANA

cover

bows

wagon bed

jockey box

tongue

reach

hounds

grease bucket

iron tire

I WALKED TO ZION

I WALKED TO ZION

True Stories of Young Pioneers
on the Mormon Trail

Susan Arrington Madsen

CINNAMON
TREE ®

PUBLISHED BY
DESERET BOOK COMPANY
SALT LAKE CITY, UTAH

In Loving Memory of Daniel Eric Madsen

Library of Congress Cataloging-in-Publication Data

Madsen, Susan Arrington
   I walked to Zion : true stories of young pioneers on
the Mormon trail / by Susan Arrington Madsen.
     p. cm.
   Includes index.
   ISBN 0-87579-848-9
   1. Mormon Trail—Juvenile literature. 2. Youth—Travel—Mormon
Trail—Juvenile literature. 3. Children—Travel—Mormon Trail—
Juvenile literature. 4. Frontier and pioneer life—Mormon Trail—
Juvenile literature. [1. Mormons—History. 2. Mormon Trail.
3. Frontier and pioneer life—Mormon Trail. 4. Children's
writings.] I. Title.
F593.M26   1994
917.804'2—dc20   94-404
                                        CIP
                                        AC

Printed in the United States of America

10   9   8   7   6   5   4

CONTENTS

Contents

PREFACE

The Mormon Trail, from Winter Quarters, Nebraska, to the Great Salt Lake Valley, is more than a thousand miles long. It's hard to imagine walking a thousand miles—especially if one must walk that far as quickly as possible, before supplies run out and before the snow flies. But between 1847 and 1869, more than seventy thousand Latter-day Saint pioneers made the trek, seeking religious freedom, with most of them walking every step of the way.

Few pioneers rode in the oxen-pulled covered wagons they used. Riding was reserved for the very young, the very old, and those too sick to take another step. The load had to be kept as light as possible for the patient but weary oxen. The Edwin D. Woolley family had a pregnant sow riding in the back of their wagon for a short time, hoping to save the piglets soon to be born. Chickens got to ride. They bounced along in small coops, tied to the sides of the wagons. But most of the courageous travelers walked to the Salt Lake Valley, arriving with sore, blistered feet. Some didn't make it at all.

Many books have been written about the westward journey of the early Latter-day Saints—often called one of the greatest epics in American history. In most of these books, however, children and teenagers are rarely seen and almost never heard. This volume takes a look at the migration from the perspective of young people who experienced the great LDS exodus.

What was the emigration experience like for those young pioneers whose eyes viewed the Mormon Trail from only three or four feet off the ground? What did they think of the journey? What did they do for fun? What were their fears? What about those who traveled without their parents? What did they think when they finally saw their dreamed-of destination—the Salt Lake Valley?

The answers to these and other questions are found in the journals and personal histories of young emigrants who crossed the Great Plains on the Mormon Trail. In preparing this book, I studied more than a hundred such sources, including ones that featured people in their late teens. In the middle 1800s, teenagers sixteen and older were generally viewed as adults, but I decided to include them because they make interesting and valuable comparisons with their peers of today. Most of the accounts I examined were written years after the incidents in them occurred—very few children or teens managed to keep a journal along the way.

To capture the magic of personal experience, I have chosen to include only first-person accounts of the trek. Who can better describe enduring the sweltering heat, the hunger, the mud, the insects or experiencing the humor and the romance of the journey than the youth who walked beside or behind the wagon? Who can better describe what was felt when a young girl was buried on the plains than her playmate who stood at the side of the shallow grave and said a last good-bye? She was there.

Only one account in this collection was written by an adult making the trek. Mary Ann Weston Maughan saw her three-year-old son, Peter, die beneath the wheels of their wagon. Her account of that experience is important in appreciating that children also made the supreme sacrifice.

For many, the journey to Zion began in their native lands far across the ocean. I have chosen to include several accounts of young people who describe leaving homes and relatives abroad and living on sailing vessels bound for America.

For readability, I have standardized spelling and punctuation, but otherwise, I have not changed wording except when necessary to clarify the meaning of a sentence. I have also deleted sentences and phrases in places not critical to the actual narrative, especially in larger chapters. In the chapter titles I have included in parentheses the future married names of the young women who made the trek because many of them are better known by those names than by their maiden names. Also, information on the photographs and illustrations may be found at the back of the book.

For the most part, these excerpts recount only the portion of the individuals' personal histories that dealt with the emigration to the Salt Lake Valley. For those desiring to read more, the title and location of the material have been provided at the end of each chapter.

Many people made this book possible. I have in particular relied on the previous research done by such excellent historians as Elliott West, University of Arkansas; Stanley B. Kimball, Southern Illinois University, and his wife, Violet; and S. George Ellsworth, Utah State University (see "References" at back of this book).

I am deeply grateful to the staff of the library and archives of the Church Historical Department in Salt Lake City, especially William Slaughter. I also appreciate the generous assistance of A. J. Simmonds and his associates in Special Collections at the Merrill Library at Utah State University.

Those who gave excellent research suggestions include my father, Leonard J. Arrington; Lyndia Carter, Oregon-California Trails Association; William G. Hartley and Richard Jensen, Joseph Fielding Smith Institute for Church History at Brigham Young University; Dorothy C. Hudman, Family History Library, Salt Lake City; Reed Durham and Kenneth Godfrey, LDS Institute of Religion in Logan; Norda Emmett; Ella Madsen; Doris Reeder; and Daina Zollinger.

I especially appreciate the valuable editing suggestions provided by Willis L. Pitkin, Jr., of the English Department at Utah State University.

James C. Jacobs, professor of children's literature at Brigham Young University, was a driving force behind this project from the very beginning. Without his encouragement and confidence, I might never have attempted this project.

As always, my friend and eternal companion, Dean, was constantly supportive, enthusiastic, and helpful. Thank you so much—teamwork means everything.

One of my wishes for our four treasured daughters, Emily, Rebecca, Sarah and Rachel, is that they will learn, as I have, to love and cherish the history of The Church of Jesus Christ of Latter-day Saints. This project has been a profound and sometimes emotional experience for me. It has increased my reverence for the human spirit and deepened my testimony of the truth of the restored gospel of Jesus Christ.

May this book serve as a reminder of the high and noble price that has been paid for the kingdom to go forth and of the ultimate joy and meaning of such sacrifice.

           ∾ SUSAN ARRINGTON MADSEN
                     HYDE PARK, UTAH
                    FEBRUARY 9, 1994

Part One
THE MORMON TRAIL

"And it shall come to pass in the last days, that the mountain of the Lord's house shall be established in the top of the mountains, and shall be exalted above the hills; and all nations shall flow unto it."

∿ ISAIAH 2:2

In 1844, Rachel Emma Woolley (Simmons) was seven years old when she was taken to the Mansion House in Nauvoo, Illinois, to view the bodies of the Prophet Joseph Smith and his brother Hyrum. Her uncle Samuel Woolley lifted her up beside the two coffins lined with black velvet, and she gazed through the hinged glass lids at the faces of those two great leaders.

Rachel was one of ten thousand mourners who solemnly filed past the two coffins to pay their last respects to the dead brothers. At her young age, Rachel could not comprehend that their deaths would change her life forever and in two years send her traveling deep into the American wilderness.

In the years up to Joseph and Hyrum's deaths, many converts had received a testimony of the restored gospel and had joined The Church of Jesus Christ of Latter-day Saints, established in western New York through Joseph Smith in 1830. But many neighbors of those who had joined this new church had often felt uneasy about the Mormon lifestyle. Quite a few were afraid the Mormons would take over the local government. Still others opposed its work.

The Latter-day Saints tried to live in Ohio, Missouri, and Illinois, but in each place they settled, members of the Church began to suffer persecutions from their neighbors. Homes and barns were burned to the ground. Crops were destroyed, and livestock stolen. Men were tarred and feathered, and people killed. In all three states, the Saints moved on to what they hoped would be more peaceful surroundings.

The largest and most successful of the early Mormon settlements had been established in 1839 on the banks of the Mississippi River. Joseph Smith named the city "Nauvoo," which meant "a beautiful and restful place." The bustling community soon boasted a population of more than twelve thousand people.

As with their previous communities, the Latter-day Saints experienced problems with anti-Mormons in neighboring communities. Joseph Smith realized they would have to leave their beautiful city. In 1842, he told the Saints they should begin to make preparations to resettle in the West, in the Rocky Mountains.

In 1844, still living in Nauvoo, Joseph and Hyrum were arrested and taken to the county jail in Carthage, Illinois. They were to be tried on a charge of riot, stemming from destruction of an anti-Mormon press, and for treason for declaring martial law. They were promised protection, but on June 27, 1844, a mob with blackened faces and loaded guns easily passed by the guards and burst into their jail cell. The mob shot and murdered the Prophet Joseph Smith and his brother Hyrum.

As time passed after Joseph's death, Church leaders realized that the time had come for the sorrowing Latter-day Saints to move on again. After careful prayer, study of maps and guides of unsettled regions in the West, and long discussions with Western explorers and trappers, leaders announced in the Church periodical *The Times and Seasons* that a "resting place" for the Saints would be found "in some good valley in the neighborhood of the Rocky Mountains."

Under the leadership of Brigham Young, the Saints would move to a place no other settlers wanted. No one would bother them there—it would be too inconvenient.

Apostle Parley P. Pratt tried to encourage the Saints by comparing the impending exodus to the transplanting of fruit trees from a small nursery to a field where they would have room to grow. "It is so with us," he said. "We want a country where we have room to expand." There would be room to grow in numbers, enlarge their settlements and farms, and live and worship as they choose. Thus began the Mormon migration to the West.

Although several hundred thousand American settlers moved west during the nineteenth century, for land, gold, or adventure, the Saints' migration was unlike any other. All were of one religious faith, united in purpose and desire. All shared the experience of leaving homes, loved ones, and friends for their religion's sake. The LDS companies were shepherded by religious leaders who rallied them when they were discouraged and chastised them when more order was necessary.

Of the entire journey from Nauvoo to the Great Salt Lake Valley, the most difficult part was the first two hundred or so miles. Increased tension between the Mormons and the governments of Illinois and the United States led to the main body of Saints leaving Nauvoo in February 1846, several weeks before they had planned to depart. Temperatures were often below freezing. The wind was bone-chilling. Under such conditions, thousands of shivering families crossed the Mississippi River into Iowa.

Later, as the great exodus continued, Apostle Wilford Woodruff described the scene on June 30 on the western side of the river as the Saints crossed the state of Iowa: "I stopped my carriage on the top of a hill in the midst of a rolling prairie where I had an extended view of all about me. I beheld the Saints coming in all directions from hills and dales, groves and prairies with their wagons, flocks, and herds, by the thousands. It looked like the movement of a nation."

After crossing Iowa, the Saints endured the winter of 1846–47 in tents, dugouts, and crude log huts in what they called Winter Quarters on the west bank of the Missouri River, in present-day Nebraska, and in other neighboring clusters of temporary settlements. More than six hundred graves in the cemetery at Winter Quarters bear testimony to the suffering these Saints endured. But this only strengthened their determination to find a permanent refuge in the Rocky Mountains.

The trek west from Winter Quarters began the following spring, on April 5, 1847, with the departure of the first wagons in Brigham Young's advance pioneer company. The Great Salt Lake was first glimpsed July 21, 1847, by an exploring party from the company, and the rest of the pioneers, including President Young, arrived in the Valley on July 24.

While the exodus from Nauvoo was taking place, and during the next twenty years, large numbers of newly converted Latter-day Saints from the eastern United States and Canada and from across the ocean in Great Britain gathered at established outfitting posts in Iowa and Nebraska, responding to their leaders' call to gather and move to the Valley. Thousands of families sold their homes and farms—often for ridiculously low prices—and loaded their wagons to join the trek.

There were many tender, heartbreaking scenes of families and friends saying goodbye to each other. Many would never see each other again. But the strength of their testimonies of the gospel made it possible for these courageous people to turn to the West and begin walking.

A lack of money was often a problem for those who wanted to join the Saints in the West. After 1849, many Latter-day Saints traveled to the Valley with help from the Perpetual Emigrating Fund. This fund loaned money to Church converts in Europe to enable them to emigrate to America and then on to Utah. Once they were established in their new homes and began to make a living, emigrants were to repay the loan, which enabled the Fund to continue its work of assistance.

The favorite vehicle for traveling across the plains was the white-topped wagon. This animal-drawn form of transportation also served as a mobile home. Families could use the wagons as kitchen and living rooms and sleep in and under them. Despite being packed with crates and barrels, the wagons were made more comfortable with oil lamps, rugs, pillows and even a little furniture. Boxes and bags of grain could be made into beds, and chests could serve as tables or chairs. Some arrangement in the wagon bed was often made for elderly or ill persons to rest, read, or knit as the vehicle bumped along the trail.

The pioneers used horses, mules, oxen, and even milk cows to pull their wagons. Oxen were the most popular, preferred not for their great speed but for their strength and durability. They were less expensive to buy than horses, and they didn't require the more expensive equipment that horses used. Instead of harnesses, simple wooden yokes around their necks would do. A person "drove" oxen by walking along the left side behind the lead oxen and using a whip or prod to urge and guide them along. They were trained to respond to shouts of "gee" (right turn) and "haw" (left turn). Under normal conditions, oxen could pull a heavily loaded wagon two miles an hour.

Many pioneers kept journals or wrote in later years about their journey. Careful study of their writings teaches us a great deal about their experiences along the Mormon Trail. The stories of young people traveling with the migrating companies are especially fascinating.

Most Mormon pioneer companies were filled with young people. Babies were held in the arms of their mothers or strapped on the back of an older sibling. Children as young as four or five trotted beside the wagon, while older brothers and sisters drove the oxen, gathered fuel for the campfires, and helped cook meals. Young teenagers frequently held the reins of teams of horses, as their fathers or mothers struggled with other duties. Older teens were expected to carry as much responsibility as the other adults. All the young people played important roles in this great migration.

These young pioneers viewed the journey across the Great Plains very differently from the adults. Some immigrant children saw their journey to the Salt Lake Valley as a delightful and exciting vacation. Alongside their family and friends, they energetically sang the songs of Zion, caught butterflies by day and fireflies at night, and learned to love the beauty and glory of the American West. Whatever fear, for example, that thirteen-year-old George Isom felt as the trip began soon vanished as he considered "the novelty of the scene, unable to recollect having ever been more than 8 or 10 miles from home." British-born Alfred Lambourne, age sixteen, could hardly contain himself the first night out on the trail: "What a delightful change it was to one city-bred to mingle in the freedom of camp life such as we enjoyed, and to pass his days under the blue canopy of heaven!" During one such clear summer evening on the Trail, April 29, 1847, two youngsters were allowed to take a peek through Orson Pratt's telescope and see Jupiter's moons.

For other youngsters, however, the Mormon Trail experience was one of pain and sorrow. Louisa Gittens (Clegg), who was fourteen, described the journey as "a long, miserable time." For many, it was a first and agonizing encounter with the reality of death. Adolescents stood in stunned silence as graves were dug for their parents, a sibling, or a beloved playmate. Laura Swenson (Fowers), age eight, watched her father die after a wagon accident. Her mother died seven days later in childbirth, leaving Laura with four younger sisters to proceed to the Salt Lake Valley as orphans. Clarence Merrill, age five, watched as his infant brother, Alonzo, died shortly after birth. Another brother, Alfred, and a sister, Amanda, died shortly thereafter "from chills and fever," and the three were buried under an oak tree.

Interestingly enough, children rarely encountered the kinds of dangers they expected. While many young people worried about Indians, wolves, and poisonous snakes, they discovered that most of their fears were unfounded.

The stories in this book show that Indians frequently worried the travelers. And indeed, there were some tragic encounters. However, Indians helped the overland travelers more than they hurt them. Sixteen-year-old George Cunningham and his family were invited to camp one night with a large group of Omaha Indians at Wood River, Nebraska. "We did so and they were very friendly," he later wrote. Eighteen-year-old Stephen Forsdick watched as a man in his company traded a pint of sugar to a Pawnee Indian for a buffalo robe. Both parties were happy with the exchange. Simpson Montgomery Molen, who was fifteen, found that the Indians usually visited their camp "demanding presents as tokens of peace and friendship" but otherwise did no harm.

One of the first Indians nine-year-old Joseph F. Smith saw "had his hair daubed up with stiff white clay." Mormons frequently met bands of Pawnee Indians. Their braves had plucked eyebrows, painted faces, and shaved heads, except for a strip of hair running from the forehead to the back of the crown, to a scalp lock at the back that looked like a horn. Children were both fascinated and frightened by the natives' war paint, weapons, and mannerisms.

Other common fears proved groundless. Wild animals were virtually no threat at all, although many children shook with fear as they lay inside a wagon at night and heard a wolf sniffing around the camp. Wolves frequently dug up graves along the Mormon Trail, leaving a ghastly scene for later travelers, but there is no reliable evidence that they posed any significant threat to the living. Rattlesnakes were a familiar sight, but snakebites were rare.

The real danger in crossing the plains was illness. Sickness killed more children than accidents, starvation, and exposure combined. Common identifiable diseases included scarlet fever, smallpox, and typhus, all communicated through personal contact. Intestinal diseases included cholera and dysentery. These painful and frightening illnesses claimed the lives of hundreds of Latter-day Saints, and children were less able than adults to withstand these scourges.

The second greatest danger to youngsters was accidents—the most common injuries being to children who fell beneath the wheels of moving wagons and handcarts. Wagon run-overs, in fact, injured or killed more children than all other kinds of accidents combined. Nervous parents tried to keep small children inside the wagons, but they soon became restless and curious and would hop in and out. Inevitably, a child would trip and hit the ground just as a wheel groaned over them. Gideon Murdock, age six, wrote, "I was not large enough to keep out of the way of the wagon at all times and consequently had my feet and leg run over two or three times when jumping out of the wagon to stop the team." Other dangers included rivers, poor nutrition, and exposure to the elements.

Despite the very real dangers the Wild West presented, most young travelers were enthralled with the new territory they were discovering. Newcomers to the West saw their first buffalo, antelope, and snow-capped mountain peaks. Mary Kristine Jacobsen (Sorensen) and her friends approached Chimney Rock, in present-day Nebraska, "with the greatest of joy and curiosity." They left their company and climbed partway up the huge, slender pillar, which she later admitted was "a very hazardous undertaking." No one is known to have successfully climbed to the top of the five-hundred-foot-high formation, but legend has it that an Indian brave, to win a bride, did reach the top, only to plunge to his death. Such landmarks as Chimney Rock, Independence Rock, and Devil's Gate broke the monotony for youngsters seeking fun and adventure.

In due time, of course, the journey came to an end. Responses upon seeing the Salt Lake Valley were mixed. Clara Decker (Young), an adult, took one look at the barren, sagebrush-blanketed valley and said, "I have come 1,200 miles to reach this valley and walked much of the way, but I am willing to walk 1,000 miles farther rather than remain here." Some voted to push on to California.

In 1866, B. H. "Harry" Roberts, who was ten, had such high expectations of his home in the Salt Lake Valley that he mistook the Bountiful LDS Tabernacle for his new house. His family's humble cottage with its sod roof and dirt floor was a bitter disappointment.

But for most, the Valley was a welcome sight, heralding not only the end of the tiresome journey but the beginning of a new life. Lucy Hannah White (Flake), who was eight years old at the time, wrote of her family's arrival in 1850: "That day happened to be Mother's thirty-second birthday, and was a joyous occasion. I couldn't understand her tears. I said: 'Mother, your loved ones are here, you wanted to come, so why are you crying?' She squeezed my hand gently, and smiling through her tears answered, 'Lucy Hannah, when people are as happy as I am, they cannot keep from crying.' That was the first time I knew that tears could express both joy and sorrow."

The accounts in this book, telling the stories of Zion's youngest pioneers, portray endurance, resilience, faith, a sense of awe, and great courage. These young people are splendid examples and models, people we can learn much from, who can teach us about crossing our own deserts and rivers and taming our own wildernesses.

SOURCES: The following journals and personal histories are used as references in Part One but are not listed elsewhere in this book:

Clegg, Louise Gittens. Autobiography. In *Our Pioneer Heritage,* compiled by Kate B. Carter, 3:87–90. 20 vols. Salt Lake City: Daughters of Utah Pioneers, 1960.

Cunningham, George. Autobiography. In *Treasures of Pioneer History,* compiled by Kate B. Carter, 5:252–56. 6 vols. Salt Lake City: Daughters of Utah Pioneers, 1956.

Flake, Lucy Hannah White. Journal, typescript. Harold B. Lee Library, Brigham Young University, Provo, Utah.

Forsdick, Stephen. Autobiography, typescript. Archives Division, Historical Department, The Church of Jesus Christ of Latter-day Saints, Salt Lake City, Utah. Hereafter cited as LDS Church Archives.

Fowers, Laura Swenson. Autobiography. In *Our Pioneer Heritage,* 12:95–97.

Isom, George. Autobiography, typescript. LDS Church Archives.

Lambourne, Alfred. *An Old Sketchbook.* Boston: Samuel E. Cassino, 1892.

Molen, Simpson Montgomery. Autobiography, holograph. LDS Church Archives.

Murdock, Gideon Allen. Autobiography, typescript. LDS Church Archives.

Sorensen, Mary Kristine Jacobsen. Oral interview with her daughter, Veda Sorensen, holograph. In possession of Daina Zollinger, River Heights, Utah.

Part Two

FUTURE LEADERS

"Now behold, a marvelous work is about to come forth among the children of men.

"Therefore, O ye that embark in the service of God, see that ye serve him with all your heart, might, mind and strength, that ye may stand blameless before God at the last day.

"Therefore, if ye have desires to serve God ye are called to the work."

❧ DOCTRINE & COVENANTS 4:1–3

The Mormon trail proved to be a testing ground and learning experience for virtually all who made the journey. It further bonded together a people who would establish hundreds of permanent settlements in the Mountain West and make it Mormon country.

Among those making the trek as youngsters were future prophets, apostles, Relief Society presidents, and other valuable leaders in the Church. To learn of the skills and testimonies they forged as young pioneers is to better understand what would later enable them to serve successfully as leaders in their communities and in The Church of Jesus Christ of Latter-day Saints.

∽

Brigham Henry Roberts

Born: March 13, 1857, Warrington, Lancashire, England
Parents: Benjamin and Ann Reed Everington Roberts
1866: William Henry Chipman Company
Age at time of journey: 10

In the above photograph, B. H. Roberts is in the disguise he used to pass through hostile territory and retrieve the bodies of two missionaries who had been shot.

"Harry" Roberts, age ten, and his sister, Mary ("Polly"), age sixteen, crossed the Great Plains with an LDS wagon train. Their father remained in England, and their mother had gone to the Salt Lake Valley four years earlier, where she was anxiously awaiting their arrival. They departed from a camp called Wyoming, which was south of Council Bluffs, Iowa, on the Nebraska side of the Missouri River, and which was on a branch of the Oregon Trail.

Captain William Henry Chipman's train was the company to which my sister and I were assigned for the journey. He was from American Fork in Utah County. The company was one of the largest leaving Missouri that year and made an imposing trail of covered wagons as it started over the long and adventurous trail. There was much cheering and cracking of whips by the teamsters and shouting of war whoops in imitation of the Indians by the Western men as they passed through the immense encampment of wagons which were to follow later in similar groups. There was a thrill in the departure for the long journey. All were rested up by the stay at the Missouri encampment, and all were eager for the march.

Soon the lack of preparation for my sister and me became manifest. Of course our clothing was sparse and by now worn and not suitable to the journey. Our mother, in distant Utah, had sent with a young teamster who came from the settlement in which she lived—Bountiful, Davis County—gloves and a shawl and stout walking shoes for Mary, with heavy quilts, homemade, for bedding and a little money, such as she could manage to scrape together. But all these comforts that would have been well-nigh invaluable for us never reached our hands. The teamster to whom our things were entrusted claimed that he could never find us in the Missouri encampments on the journey.

The only night covering I had was a petticoat that my sister Mary slipped to me after retiring into the wagon. This night covering I caught with eager hands, and I curled up under the wagon and generally shivered through the night.

On one occasion, I and a boy about my own age had become interested in some ripening yellow currants along one of the banks of the stream and lingered until the train had passed over a distant hill. Before we realized it, we were breaking camp regulations, but still we lingered to fill our hats with the luscious currants we had discovered.

The caps at last filled, we started to catch the wagon train and were further behind it than we realized.

Coming to the summit of a swale in which the wagon road passed, we saw to our horror three Indians on horseback just beginning to come up out of the swale and along the road. Our contact with the Indians around the Wyoming encampment had not been sufficient to do away with the fear in which the red men were held by us, and it could be well imagined that the hair on our heads raised as we saw an inevitable meeting with these savages.

Nevertheless, we moved one to the right and the other to the left with the hope that we could go around these Indians, but nothing doing. As soon as we separated to go around, the Indians also separated—the one to the right, the other to the left, and the third straight forward. There was trembling and fear that we were going to be captured. It was, therefore, with magnificent terror that we kept on slowly towards these Indians whose faces remained immobile and solemn with no indication of friendliness given out at all.

I approached my savage, knowing not what to do, but as I reached about the head of the horse, I gave one wild yell, the Scotch cap full of currants was dropped, and I made a wild dash to get by—and did—whereupon there was a peal of laughter from the three Indians. They say Indians never laugh, but I learned differently. As the race for the train continued with an occasional glance over the shoulder to see what the Indians were doing, I saw they were bending double over their horses with their screams of laughter.

The running continued until each of us had found his proper place beside the wagon to which he was assigned. The fright was thought of for several days, at least by strict adherence to camp rules about staying with your wagon.

One morning, Harry heard the company was going to cross the Platte River (probably near Ft. Kearney, Nebraska) for the first time to pick up the Mormon Trail of 1847. He wanted to be the first in the company to arrive at the crossing, so he walked on ahead of the rest of his group.

Up the stream, probably one quarter of a mile where a side stream dipped into the Platte, clumps of willows grew, and as the sun by now was burning hot, I thought of the grateful shade that could be reached by going that far above the point where the road dipped into the river. I went on and soon found a comfortable place where I could recline and dropped into a sound slumber that had been denied me the night before on account of the cold.

I slept on and on, and not all the shouting of the teamsters and emigrants nor the lunging of the wagons into the river awoke me. In fact, when I did awake, the last wagon of the train was just pulling up the opposite bank of the river, where the road led into the cottonwoods and other river trees, and was winding up the opposite bank of the turbid stream. Shouting at the top of my voice and rushing down to where the road met the river, I attracted the attention of Captain Chipman, who sat upon his horse on the opposite bank, watching the last wagon as it was drawn from the river bed by its long line of yoked teams. Cupping his hands the captain shouted to know if I could swim and was answered in the affirmative.

I was directed to "come on then." With this, my old clogs [wooden shoes] from England were shuffled off blistered feet and left on the sand bar. Slipping off my coat—made as will be remembered from an old suit of a policeman, thick and heavy—with only shirt and barn-door trousers left, I plunged through one stream after another between the sandbars until I came to the main stream, which surged to the north side of the Platte above which on the bank sat Captain Chipman. Without hesitation I plunged into this last stream, to be carried down very rapidly. Apparently Captain Chipman felt uneasy and drove his horse, well practiced, into the stream and came swimming to where I was struggling for the further shore. The captain slipped his foot from the stirrup and bade me take hold of it, and the horse without being turned upstream swam down until a suitable landing place was reached, and all three of us came up from the river together. The Captain held in his hand a light horse whip, and as I let go of the stirrup and scampered up the bank to reach the road, the captain felt it evidently not unjust to give several sharp cuts cross my pants, which stung sharply, but no cry was uttered, and I felt that I was well out of a bad scrape.

During another crossing of the Platte River, Harry and a young lady in the camp secretly rode in the back of a wagon that became stuck in quicksand midway across the river. After several attempts were made to free the wagon, the team of horses was unhitched and taken to the other side of the river until another, stronger team could be brought in. Meanwhile, the following incident took place while Harry and the young girl waited for help:

A team did not return until the next morning, and all through the night the vibrations of the wagon in the sand were continued until the water reached and seeped into the bed of the wagon and soaked the sugar bags. Hunger, of course, asserted itself, and how to satisfy it for the time was the question. But I was carrying as my most precious possession a four-bladed pen knife, a gift for my mother, which had been purchased with money coming into my hands in England. In addition to the four blades there were a pair of pinchers, a nail file, and some other contrivances that made it an amateur tool chest. The knife was used to slit a hole in one of the sacks of sugar; one of the pieces of side bacon was uncovered in the same way, and pieces of raw bacon or ham were hacked off. Upon these the young lady and I feasted.

While cutting the bacon, the knife slipped and dropped into the turbid water of the Platte River and was never found, and the treasure which had been bought for my mother, who was remembered to be a seamstress and to whom the complex knife and other implements would have been useful, was gone forever.

The next morning teams were brought to the relief of the freight wagons, of which there were several, which had been left in the river bed from the day before. It was always a matter of regret that the young lady's name was either never learned or else not remembered.

On one occasion a night drive was necessary, and a young man was entrusted with the freight wagon team. The young teamster was unusually devoted to helping the young ladies, especially on this night, so I ran in behind the ox on the near side and climbed up on the seat that had been arranged in the front of the wagon by the regular teamsters. This seat consisted of a broad plank placed across the open head of a large barrel. The day had been hot and the hours of the journey long, and I was decidedly tired, nearly unto exhaustion. Fearing that my riding, which was "agin" the law, would be discovered, I slipped the broad board from the barrel head and conceived the idea of dropping down in the barrel, secure from the eyes of those who might oust me from my seat in the wagon if I were found. To my surprise, if not amazement, I discovered when I let myself down in the barrel that my feet went into about three or four inches of a sticky liquid substance which turned out to be molasses. The smarting of my chapped feet almost made me scream with pain, but I stifled it. Too tired to attempt to climb out, I remained and gradually slipped down and went to sleep doubled up in the bottom of the barrel, with such results as can well be imagined. It was daylight when I woke up, and there began to be the usual camp noises of teamsters shouting to each other to be prepared to receive the incoming team driven from the prairie by night herdsmen. As I crawled out of the uncomfortable position, and with molasses dripping from my trousers, I was greeted with yells and laughter by some of the teamsters and emigrants who caught sight of me. I crept away as fast as I could to scrape off the syrup, which added to the weight and thickness of shirt and trousers, for there was no change of clothing for me, and so bedaubed I had to pass on until dusk and drying somewhat obliterated the discomfort.

The lads in the train were always in search of swimming holes, so they scampered down through the willows in search of bathing places. I and a comrade more venturesome than the rest went some distance down the stream until we found a swimming hole that was admirable. The water had washed out a hole on the west side of the creek with quite a deep clear collection of water under the banks held up by the willow roots. Here we began our bath. Cattle were on both sides of the streams when suddenly a strange rattling sound was heard, followed by intense hissing and hissing. Looking out of the swimming hole, we observed three Indians riding up the bank of the stream. One of them had a dry piece of rawhide in his hand, which by shaking produced the rattling noise. All three, following the rattling of the rawhide, hissed intensely. As they did so, the cattle with loud bawling rushed out of the willows to the open prairie, which rolled off in successive hills. Pretty soon it seemed as if the whole herd, whose thundering hoofs could be heard, were stampeded, their mad race accompanied with bawlings. The thundering of their hoofs would have waked the dead.

As soon as the Indians and cattle had reached the creek bottom, we, naked as when born, ran for camp full speed. We found Captain Chipman seated on the tongue of his wagon and made our report of the Indians among the cattle, apparently stampeding them. The captain laughed at us and advised that we had better find our clothes before we went into camp. While saying this, he climbed upon the tongue of his wagon and opened the lid to his bread box in front, making an improvised seat of it. As he did this, it enabled the captain to see over a line of willows, and he beheld the whole herd under stampede, followed by the three Indians. All at once a cry arose from the encampment, a number of whom now saw the cattle under stampede. Then there were attempts of mounting in hot haste and seizure of firearms and a rush made to follow the marauders. Captain Chipman, however, stood at the west entrance of the encampment and commanded all to remain where they were until he could give his orders. We two boys, meantime, wended our way back to the swimming hole, where we obtained our clothing.

Captain Chipman here proved himself a real plainsman captain, and the thought nearest his heart was care for the emigrants bound on their way to Zion. He ordered the men to roll up the wagons into solid corral formation, namely by pushing the wagons together in such manner as to have the forewheel pushed up and interlocked with the hind wheels of the wagon before it. The corral became an improvised fort, with the men and the women of the camp and such stock as remained huddled on the inside. After this the three remaining horses of the encampment were brought out and saddled, and three men mounted and went after the Indians to bring back as many of the herd as would be possible.

As a result of this incident, the company lost over one hundred head of their strongest and best cattle and six or eight riding horses. The men were able to bring home only a very few of the herd.

It was the custom of the emigrants to gather and carry in their arms, or else in the rear of their wagon, dry sticks gathered from the bushes or else "Buffalo Chips" from the plains for the evening camp fires. "Buffalo Chips" were the droppings of cattle and buffaloes that once inhabited the region in certain seasons of the year, and these "dried chips" made an excellent smoldering fire that gave out a great amount of heat.

Before dark, I had gathered my quantum of such fuel. Then the train was drawn up in such formation as the usual corral. I wandered outside the corral a bit until I found two boulder stones, which I rolled together. Between the two I lighted my fire, carrying a blazing buffalo chip from another fire with which to ignite this fire. After it had burned down a little, I curled myself about the two stones with the fire between, and in the warmth sleep soon overcame me. In the early morning when I awoke, to my amazement I was covered with an inch or two of snow which had fallen through the night and which had covered me and my now dead fire, as with a white blanket. Shaking off the snow, I made my way to look for breakfast, grateful for this long night of pleasant and apparently warm covering until the sharpness of the morning hour made me shiver again with cold.

Before long, we approached Chimney Rock, Nebraska, which had a peculiar attraction to Mary and me because it was at this point that our baby brother, Thomas, who had been carried from the Missouri River in the arms of our mother, had died and was buried. To us it was, in a way, his monument. The child had been afflicted from its birth with water on the brain, and the head had grown large with the progress of the disease. He was peevish and during the whole journey did not permit anyone to touch him but his mother, and here this burden had ended.

There was a pathetic painful incident in his burial. Morton B. Haight was the captain of the company in which my mother made the journey, in the year 1862. The grave for the baby was dug between Chimney Rock and the Platte River, and the babe wrapped in a blanket, a bed sheet, and lowered into the grave. Then came the dropping of the dirt upon the body. This was too much for my mother, and with a groan she sank beside the grave in a dead faint, as she heard the clods of dirt fall upon her baby's body. "Hold on," said the captain, beginning to feel the grief, "this is too much for me." He went to his wagon and took out the bread box in the front end of it and came back with it to the grave. Then the body was taken up and comfortably placed in the bread box and in this improvised coffin was again lowered to the bottom of the grave, which was then filled in and covered with cobblestones gathered from the surrounding hills to afford protection. Ever after, of course, the name of Captain Haight was an enshrined memory in the Roberts house.

Harry describes their arrival in the Great Salt Lake Valley on September 14, 1866:

In the morning everybody seemed to be up with the first streaks of the light of day over the eastern mountains, and in great haste in preparation to take up the journey. Breakfast seemed to be neglected, and there was not much to eat anyway. Before the sun rose, the train, falling into its old line, swung down the low foothills until they struck a well-defined road leading into the city.

This entrance proved to be via Third South—then and long afterwards known as "Emigration Street," now Broadway. When Captain Chipman's ox team swung around the corner of Third South into Main Street, I found myself at the head of the lead yoke in that team, walking up the principal street of the city, the rest of the train following. Here the people had turned out to welcome the plains-worn emigrants and were standing on the street sides to greet them. Some horsemen dashed up the street swinging their cowboy hats, the customary cowboy handkerchiefs around their necks as if they were in from the ranges.

Along the road, perhaps nearly halfway from the mouth of Parley's Canyon to the city, as I strode on ahead of Captain Chipman's team, I saw a bright-colored, dainty, charming little girl approaching me in the middle of the street. It was a strange meeting, we two. My hair had grown out somewhat. But three months' journey over the plains and through the mountains without hat or coat or shoes for most of the way had wrought havoc with my appearance. My hair stuck out in all directions; the freckles seemed deeper and more plentiful and the features less attractive than when the journey began. Shirt and trousers barely clung to my sturdy form, and my feet were black and cracked but now covered by the shoes I had taken from the feet of a dead man at a burnt station. These I was wearing in compliment to my entrance into "Zion." Also my face had been more carefully washed that morning.

But try as I would, the shock of hair was unmanageable, and so no wonder the dainty little lady was somewhat timid in approaching me. She had on her arm a basket of luscious fruit, peaches, plums, and grapes. These she extended to me, the "ugly duckling" of a boy from the plains, and asked me if I would have some peaches. The answer was to gather up several which I strung along in the crook of my arm, and as soon as I had obtained what I supposed a reasonable portion, I wondered how I could get this fruit so wonderful back to Mary and at the same time retain my place in the march up Main Street. Pondering this question, of course unknown to the young girl who had brought me such a treasure, I finally turned back as best I could to the wagon where Mary was concealed under the wagon cover because of her being a little ashamed of her appearance. Running behind the wheel ox and climbing up on the tongue of the wagon, I called to my sister, handed to her the fruit, and then scrambled back to the ground and ran for my place at the head of the train and marched on until the head of Main Street was reached.

This then was the old tithing office behind the high cobble walls with its half-round bastions and through a crude gateway on the west side of the block leading into the stock corrals of President Young, where most of the wagons of the train were driven and placed under the many straw-covered sheds that then occupied the place where the Deseret Gymnasium now stands. The cattle were soon freed from the yoke and seemed delighted with the straw and hay brought them.

Across the way on Temple Square block, the foundations of the temple rose above the general level of the surrounding ground and seemed to be an object of interest to nearly all the emigrants, many of whom were permitted to go within the wall and view it. By and by there were numerous meetings in various groups of people, friends of the emigrants, parents, and sweethearts, and perhaps in some instances wives of the teamsters that had returned. There seemed to be an air of cheerfulness in all this meeting of people on the arrival of this large emigrant train of Saints.

Mary and I seemed to be so little part of this excitement and joy, because nobody seemed to come for us. Mary remained concealed under the wagon cover, and I, lonesome and heartsick, sat upon the tongue of Captain Chipman's wagon, my chin in my hands and elbows upon my knees, thinking "Zion" was not so much after all, if this was all of it. The spirit of sadness, if it was not forlornness, settled upon me.

Presently, however, approaching from the west gate, I saw a woman in a red and white plaid shawl slowly moving among the hillocks of fertilizer that had been raked from the sheds and the yard. She seemed to be daintily picking her way, and there was something in the movement of her head as she looked to the right and to the left that seemed familiar to me. The woman was moving in my direction, and the closer she came the stronger the conviction grew upon me that there was my mother. I would have known her from the dainty cleanliness of everything about her.

I stood until she came nearly parallel to where I sat; then sliding from the tongue of the wagon, I said, "Hey Mother," and she looked down upon my upturned face. Without moving she gazed upon me for some time and at last said, "Is this you, Harry? Where is Mary?" Of course Mary was in the wagon, and I led my mother to where she was hiding, and when mother and daughter met, there was a flood of tears on both sides. At last I joined them, making the trio of the united family. It seemed difficult for our mother to realize that we at last were her children after more than four years of separation, but once in a while, a smile would break through the tears and she seemed to be extremely happy. A neighbor of hers, Brother John K. Crosby, a New Englander, had driven her from Bountiful to the city to get us children, and it took but a short time to leave the remaining emigrant teams and people to find this wagon and make the start for home, Bountiful.

There was one thing remembered in this reunion, and that was on my part. I felt that I had arrived, that I belonged to somebody, that somebody had an interest in me, and these were the thoughts that were in my mind as I sat in the wagon on the drive home to Bountiful.

❧

Harry later became known as B. H. Roberts, who became a president of the First Council of the Seventy at the age of thirty-one. He was elected to the United States Congress, and he became a prolific writer of theology and history. Elder Roberts married Sarah Louise Smith, Celia Louisa Dibble, and Margaret Curtis, and was the father of fifteen children. He died September 27, 1933, in Salt Lake City.

SOURCE: B. H. Roberts. *The Autobiography of B. H. Roberts,* edited by Gary James Bergera, 25–44. Salt Lake City: Signature, 1990. Note: B. H. Roberts used third person pronouns (he, him, his) in his account when referring to himself. Bergera has changed them to first person (I, me, my).

Aurelia Read Spencer (Rogers)

Born: October 4, 1834, Deep River, Middlesex, Connecticut
Parents: Orson and Catherine Cannon Curtis Spencer
1848: Brigham Young Company
Age at time of journey: 13

Aurelia and five younger siblings crossed the plains without their parents. Their father was serving a mission in England at the time, editing the Millennial Star, *a Mormon periodical. Their mother had died in the severe cold as the Saints were driven from Nauvoo, Illinois.*

We left Winter Quarters about the first of May, 1848, traveling in President Young's company.

On this journey I met and became acquainted with Thomas Rogers, who afterwards became my husband. He drove a team for Andrew Cahoon, who was captain of our ten; the company was divided into tens and fifties.

During the journey the company would stop once in a while for a few days to recruit their teams and give the women a chance to wash, iron, bake, etc.

On one of these occasions, we camped on Looking-Glass Creek, Nebraska, which emptied into the Platte River about a mile below. The people had been counseled not to go far from camp; but either forgetting or not heeding the counsel, about a dozen girls, myself included, took it into our heads, one bright moonlight night, to go to the mouth of the creek and bathe in the river, thinking the distance would make us safe from interruption. The Platte River was very wide in places, and the water quite shallow, being interspersed with sand bars. The company forded it many times in the course of their travels.

One elderly lady, namely Sister Mima Young, generally called Aunt Mima, went with us as a protector, or to stand guard while we should take our bath. A nice place was selected, and we were soon splashing around in the water as happy as could be.

Presently one of the girls said, "Let us play baptize." Some of the rest consented and were soon ducked under the water, although I don't remember that any ceremony was used. We were soon interrupted in our sport, however, by some one exclaiming, "See! what is that? What is coming?" All looked in the direction pointed out, and sure enough something white and strange looking was coming, right towards us across the river, and only a short distance away. Then such a screaming and rushing for the shore were perhaps never witnessed before nor since, some of the girls almost falling down in the water from fright. I was like one paralyzed, could not speak or move for a few seconds, and was nearly the last one out of the water. But all gained the shore in safety; looking back we saw the object which had so frightened us go up the creek and disappear.

Our conjectures were varied in regard to what it might have been; some thought it much larger than it seemed to others. But whatever it was, it floated towards us until we started for the shore, then turned and went up the creek. All agreed that it was a warning, and felt that we had done wrong in playing baptize.

We wended our way back to the wagons quite sobered, reflecting and talking these things over as we went along; but the mystery of what we had seen was never solved.

❧

Aurelia Spencer married Thomas Rogers March 27, 1851, and they lived in Farmington, Utah. They became the parents of twelve children. It was Aurelia who first suggested the Church start an organization for children. Her idea was accepted by President John Taylor, and the Primary was organized. She became president of the first Primary, organized on August 25, 1878, in Farmington, Utah. In recognition of her role in founding the Primary, the children of the Church raised funds to publish her book Life Sketches *in 1898. Aurelia died August 19, 1922, at the age of eighty-seven. She is buried in Salt Lake City, Utah.*

Source: Aurelia Spencer Rogers. *Life Sketches of Orson Spencer and Others, and History of Primary Work,* 76–79. Salt Lake City: George Q. Cannon & Sons, 1898.

RUTH MAY (FOX)

Born: November 16, 1853, Westbury, Wiltshire, England
Parents: James and Mary Ann Harding May
1867: Leonard G. Rice Company
Age at time of journey: 13

Whatever the reason, when the time came for our departure from England, I was in the seventh heaven. The lady who was to be my stepmother, and her daughter—who was about my own age—and myself left our home under cover of darkness to avoid the curiosity of the neighbors. Could anything be more thrilling?

After a walk of four or five miles under the stars, we boarded the train to Liverpool, England. Arriving there, some necessities had to be purchased. Then came the novelty of climbing into a great steamship. To stand on a floating city and gradually pull away from the wharf with hundreds of people waving their hats or handkerchiefs in a fond adieu and hearty "God-speed you" is an event never to be forgotten.

We had secured berths in the steerage, which meant that we must descend through a trap door to our quarters below the deck. The sleeping accommodations consisted of a large shelf or platform on either side of the vessel, which, by means of boards, could be divided into spaces just large enough to accommodate one person. If a family preferred to sleep closer together, the boards could be removed, thus giving more room and per-haps more comfort, if comfort could be thought of under such conditions.

As I remember, there was absolutely no privacy, no provision even to hang up a pair of hose for protection from the eyes of the curious. On the same level were great long tables where we sat to eat our meals, the usual menu being soup, rice, hardtack, and sour biscuits.

It happened that an old gentleman from Lancashire, England, and his wife occu-pied berths next to ours. For at least half an hour before the soup was served, he would entertain himself and annoy the rest of us by hammering his hardtack into little bits so that it would eventually absorb sufficient soup to make its passage down the esophagus more easily.

Near the end of our trip what's that we hear? Oh joy, "Land in sight!" Now for thrills! Everybody must see land and joyously watch the vessel going nearer and nearer to the shore. But things must be gathered up and packed. Trunks must be brought up from the hold. Good-byes must be spoken. Everybody is busy and excited, each vying with the other in seeing who shall leave the old ship first. At last we landed at Castle Garden, New York, and there we must stay until friends or relatives learn that the *Louisiana* is in port. It was late evening and quite dark save for the lamplight when through the crowd I heard my father say, "There she is. Bless her dear little face."

We soon moved to Philadelphia and found employment. My wage was a dollar a week and board. Thus we began to save and prepare for the journey to the Valley.

In July, 1867, we started for North Platte, which was then the terminal of the railroad and the outfitting place for those who were going West. We had to change trains at Niagara Falls and to our delight had a few hours' stay near that awe-inspiring torrent, which is forever dashing over the brink to the foaming depths below.

One night we spent on a cattle boat sailing up the Missouri River. The cattle, judging from their bellowing, seemed not to enjoy our company any better than we enjoyed theirs.

When we arrived at North Platte, it so happened that a certain brother had a wagon and one yoke of cattle, so the bargain was made that Father join his cattle to this outfit and drive all the way for his share in the wagon. The owner of the outfit had a wife and seven children. Our little family consisted of five, as Father was bringing a little girl across the plains to join her relatives in Salt Lake City. So you see there were fourteen persons with all their worldly possessions in that one wagon. The owners of the wagon used it for a sleeping apartment, and my father bought a small tent, just large enough for the five of us to lie down in side by side, like sardines in a can.

Imagine if you can these would-be drivers, who had, perhaps, never seen a Texas steer before, go through the procedure for the first time of yoking their cattle. Truly no rodeo could match the scene. The men had to be instructed in this art, and some did not learn very quickly. The same was true of the use of firearms. Every man was supposed to have his own gun and ammunition, though he had never fired a shot in his life.

With everything in readiness, the command is given and our sixty wagons—fifty of them belonging to Scandinavian Saints—are on the way, and we could sing:

> *We've left the realms of Babylon and*
> *crossed the mighty seas;*
> *We've left the good old ship where we*
> *walked about at ease.*
> *And now's the time for starting boys,*
> *We'll jog on if you please.*

So gee up; my lads. Gee whoa! Push
on my lads, Heigh Ho!
For there's none can lead a life like we
Merry Mormons do.

Other than one birth and an accidental death by a bullet when men were shooting sage hens, our journey across the plains seems to have been rather lacking in perilous adventure but was always interesting.

We camped where there were trees and water. I do not remember the name of the place, but I do remember this incident: It was quite late at night when one of the brethren thought he could hear someone stealthily moving among the bushes. You must know that everyone was a little watchful of Indians. So this brother took out his pistol and three times he gave the warning, "Speak or I'll shoot! Speak or I'll shoot! Speak or I'll shoot!" and then off went the gun. This, however, caused some merriment as it was discovered later that it was merely the wind playing with the leaves.

The Platte is a very winding river, so we crossed it many times without much inconvenience as the Scandinavian brothers would take us girls on their backs and carry us cross the stream.

One night we pitched our tent in this sand, when lo the wind blew and the rain descended and beat upon that tent, and great was the fall thereof. Mother hurried to the wagon of a friend, and we girls held up the tent while father tried to drive in the pins, which was an almost hopeless task. However, as we trudged along the next day we sang lustily:

We may get wet a little when we have a
shower of rain,
The heat may skin our noses, but they'll
soon get well again.
And when we think of Zion's land, we'll
forget the wet and pain
So, Gee up! My lads. Gee whoa!
Push on my lads, Heigh Ho!

There's none can lead a life like we
Merry Mormons do.

Chimney Rock, in Nebraska, and Independence Rock, in Wyoming, had both contributed to our recreational activity, but no one but those who have walked over prairies and deserts for days, where water is so scarce that the creeks were reduced to little puddles of alkali water, can imagine the beauty and glory of a river! On the Sweetwater we rested, washed our clothing, went in bathing, and had a real jollification.

On one of these few and far between occasions, father being very tired, having walked every step of the way, after he had unyoked his cattle, threw himself on the ground to rest, when one of the brethren came along and asked, "Well, Brother May, how are you today?" Father answered quickly, "Oh! There isn't much the matter—I have a sick wife, two sore heels, and two dummies, that's all." I was one of the dummies.

At Echo Canyon we were joined by a couple of boys whose home was in Goshen. These lads offered to ride us girls through this rugged freak of nature, so lickety split we came down the narrow defile, expecting every minute to be thrown from the rickety old light wagon and killed. This afforded great sport for the boys, who knew no fear of the canyon and saw no dangers, but to emigrants who had never before seen such a sight, it was breath-taking, to say the least.

Our last pull was through Parley's Canyon and up to the top of the hill. This was accomplished at twilight, and here we got our first glimpse of the little city of Salt Lake.

I have to admit some disappointment as I exclaimed: "Oh, have we come all this way for that?" We continued on to the campground that night. Next morning was the Sabbath.

The sky was blue and radiant, the valley fair, and the grand old mountains proudly guarded the home of the prophets. The family took a bath in a wash basin, put on our best clothes, and went to the tabernacle services. My dreams came true, and all was well in Zion.

❧

Ruth May married Jesse Williams Fox on May 8, 1873, when she was nineteen. They became the parents of twelve children. She served as General President of the Young Women's Mutual Improvement Association (YWMIA) from 1929 to 1937. Ruth May Fox was active in many political and civic organizations, including the Utah Woman Suffrage Association, and she helped draft the suffrage clause of the Utah Constitution. She died on April 12, 1958, in Salt Lake City at the age of 104.

Source: Ruth May Fox. "From England to Salt Lake Valley in 1867." *The Improvement Era* 38, no. 7 (July 1935): 406–9, 450.

JOSEPH F. SMITH

Born: November 13, 1838, Far West, Caldwell County, Missouri
Parents: Hyrum and Mary Fielding Smith
1848: Heber C. Kimball Company
Age at time of journey: 9

Joseph F. Smith's father, Hyrum Smith, was an older brother of the Prophet Joseph Smith, and both he and Joseph were murdered in 1844 in Carthage, Illinois. Joseph F. helped his widowed mother across the plains, yoking and unyoking the oxen and carefully guiding the animals over many dangerous trails.

In the spring of 1848, as the Presidency and all who were able were leaving Winter Quarters for the Valley, my mother made an attempt to go along. During the fall and winter she had made two trips down into Missouri to purchase provisions and trade for "necessities" for the family, which numbered in all, about eleven.

Once I accompanied her, along with my uncle Joseph Fielding, at which time we went to St. Joseph, Missouri, and purchased corn and had it ground at Savannah, and on our way home we camped in the edge of a wood, in the neighborhood of a large herd of cattle that were being driven to market. In the morning our best yoke of cattle were gone. My uncle and I hunted far and near but could not find them. We enquired of the herdsmen and followed their directions but could not find our oxen. This broke up our team so that we could not travel and would have been under the necessity of purchasing or trading in some way for another yoke before we could have moved on.

But after some delay, and Mother had cleared up after breakfast, she started out to find the cattle. Uncle thought it was useless for her to go. I confess I thought so too, but I had more faith that she would find them, if findable, than I had in either my or my uncle's finding them. While Mother was walking along through the tall grass, one of the herdsmen rode up to her and said he had seen her cattle over in the opposite direction to what she was going. Strange to say she passed right on, not heeding what had been said at all. He repeated, she paid no attention but passed on as tho' she were in "the strait and narrow path." Suddenly she came upon a slight ravine filled with tall willows, and in a dense cluster of large willows she found the oxen, where they had been fastened up during the night by the herdsmen with the intention of stealing them and driving them to the market, for they were in good condition. After the cattle were found, these worthy herdsmen suddenly rode off, perhaps in search of honesty, which I trust they found.

We moved on smoothly until we reached a point about midway between the Platte and Sweetwater Rivers. One of our best oxen lay down in the yoke as if poisoned, and all supposed he would die. Captain Lott now blustered about, as if the world was about at an end. "There," he said. "I told you you would have to be helped, and that you would be a burden on the company." But in this he was mistaken, for after praying for the ox and pouring oil upon him, he got up and we drove along, only detaining the company a very short time.

We had not gone far when another fell down like the first. But with the same treatment he got up as the other. I believe this was repeated the third time, to the astonishment of all who saw and the chagrin of Captain Lott.

My team leaders' names were Thom and Joe—we raised them from calves, and they were both white. Thom was trim built, active, young, and more intelligent than many a man. Many times while traveling sandy or rough roads, on long, thirsty drives, my oxen were lowing with the heat and fatigue. I would put my arms around Thom's neck and cry bitter tears! That was all I could do. Thom was my favorite and best and most willing and obedient servant and friend. He was choice!

~

Joseph F. Smith arrived in the Salt Lake Valley on September 23, 1848, along with his mother, his sister Martha Ann, and other extended family members. He served a mission at the unusually young age of fifteen to the Hawaiian Islands. He eventually had a large family of six wives and forty-eight children (five were adopted). Elder Joseph F. Smith became an apostle at the age of twenty-seven, and in 1901 he became the sixth President of The Church of Jesus Christ of Latter-day Saints. President Smith died November 19, 1918, in Salt Lake City, Utah. He was eighty years old.

SOURCE: Joseph F. Smith. Reminiscent account, holograph. In Joseph F. Smith Papers. Used by special permission of the LDS Church Archives.

Part Three
HANDCARTS

"No person can describe it, nor could it be comprehended or understood by any human living in this life, but those who were called to pass through it."

～ JOURNAL OF JENS NEILSON
MEMBER, JAMES G. WILLIE HANDCART COMPANY

By 1856, the expense of outfitting several thousand immigrants each year with covered wagons and livestock was becoming too great for the pioneers and for the Church. Leaders decided to furnish immigrants with small two-wheeled carts, close in size to those used by apple peddlers in Eastern cities, which could be pulled and pushed by hand to the Salt Lake Valley.

Although the Latter-day Saints did not invent this method of crossing the plains (some gold-rushers had used wheelbarrows and handcarts as early as 1850), their development of this method became the most remarkable travel experiment in the settlement of the American frontier.

The vehicle required no time-consuming harnessing and no concern for maintenance of livestock. Each cart carried provisions and a few personal effects for four or five people. Wagons accompanying the train transported heavier belongings, one wagon for each twenty handcarts.

The idea seemed so practical that nineteen hundred people signed up for the handcart immigration in 1856, traveling by train from the ports of Boston and New York City to Iowa City, Iowa, where the handcarts were waiting. Later, the railroad would go as far west as the Missouri River, making it a new departure point. There, immigrants were then organized into companies of one hundred carts.

The handcart era lasted only five years, bringing about three thousand Saints to the Valley. Out of the ten handcart companies that were organized, eight arrived safely and with little difficulty. Two companies in 1856, however, under the leadership of James G. Willie and Edward Martin, started too late and suffered terrible hardships in early winter storms in Wyoming. Rescue teams were sent out from Salt Lake City, but they did not arrive in time to prevent many deaths from exposure and malnutrition. Of the approximately one thousand immigrants in these two companies, more than two hundred died.

Small though their total numbers were, the three thousand handcart pioneers carved a monument of legendary proportions in the minds and hearts of the entire Mormon people.

∽

Peter Howard McBride

Born: May 3, 1850, Rothsay, Isle of Butte, Scotland
Parents: Robert and Margaret Ann Howard McBride
1856: Edward Martin Handcart Company
Age at time of journey: 6

In above photograph, Peter McBride with wife, Ruth, and their baby, Robert Franklin.

In the year 1856 my parents decided to emigrate to America, as they had heard that it was a wonderful place to live. They sold their good comfortable home and in May of that year embarked on the good ship *Horizon*. After leaving our home in Southport, Scotland, we visited with my mother's people and were not treated very kindly by them. My grandfather said, "I never want to see you again. If you should write, your letters will be burned before we read them. I hope you will all be swallowed up in the ocean before you land on that American shore. You bring disgrace to the family name by joining such a cursed church."

The McBride family went by train to Liverpool, England, and then crossed the ocean. They traveled by train to Iowa City, Iowa, where they were assigned handcarts with which to cross the Great Plains.

We had to burn buffalo chips for wood, not a tree in sight, no wood to be found anywhere. Just dry earth and rivers. We children and old folks would start early so we wouldn't be too far behind at night. A great many handcarts broke down, oxen strayed away, which made traveling rather slow. Quite an undertaking to get nearly one thousand persons who had never had any camping experience to travel, eat, and cook over campfires. It took much patience for the captain to get them used to settling down at night and to get started in the morning.

We saw a great many buffalo as we traveled up the Platte River. The people were forbidden to kill them, as it made the Indians angry. So they hired the Indians to kill what they needed to eat. An Indian sold a man a whole buffalo for five cents' worth of tobacco. Both parties were satisfied. Sometimes a herd of fifty thousand buffalo would cross the plains, and one time our company met three thousand Sioux Indians, all warriors all in war paint. Our people were much frightened, fear held the whole camp in its grip as they all expected to be annihilated. But their fears were groundless. They told our interpreters they were going to fight the Pawnee tribes. They wouldn't hurt us because we were mostly squaws and papooses. It would be cowardly to fight us, so they gave us the road.

Much hunger and cold were experienced by these weary handcart travelers; all they had to eat was a little flour, which was cut to 3/4 pound to a person. Many aged people died; even the young people could not stand the hardships. My baby sister and I were even cut to less flour, and we were really hungry. Our teams gave out and died, and we were glad to eat the meat. I remember some men passed us one day and stopped to talk. They gave my baby sister some cookies. She carried them in her little pocket, and I was always with her and would tease for a bite. She would give me a taste once in a while, and it was so good. No cake I ever tasted since was ever so good. The exposure to cold rain, snow, and ice, pushing carts all day, the scarcity of food and wood caused many strong men to perish.

A man by the name of Cyrus Wheelock, just returning from a mission to the Eastern States, was riding a horse. He carried some of the children across the river, even helped pull some of the handcarts by a rope fastened to his saddle. One time he had three little boys on his horse, one in front and two behind him. I was the last boy on that side of the river and tried to wade across. He told me to climb up behind the last boy behind his saddle, which I did. We crossed the river all right, then the horse leaped up the steep bank, and I slid off in the shallow water. I held on to the horse's tail and came out all right.

That night the wind was blowing very cold, and the carts were sheltered behind a big bluff, but the snow drifted in and covered our tent. My father died that night. He had worked hard all day pushing and pulling handcarts through the icy waters of that dangerous river, helping many people with all their belongings to reach the other side.

When Peter saw them bury his father, he ran out and started crying. Someone stopped him and tried to console him about his father's death. He cried more. He walked to the place where they had buried him and said, "My father had my fish hooks in his pocket and I want them."

My mother was sick all the way over, and my sister Jenetta had the worry of us children. She carried water from the river to do the cooking. Her shoes gave out, and she walked through the snow barefoot, actually leaving bloody tracks in the snow. Father was a good singer. He had charge of the singing in our company, and the night he died he sang a song, the first verse that reads "O Zion, when I think of you, I long for pinions like a dove, And mourn to think I should be so distant from the land I love."

We camped at the Sweetwater River. A meeting was held. It was decided that we could go no further, the snow so deep and no food. We were doomed to starvation.

They gave me a bone of an ox that had died. I cut off the skin and put the bone in the fire to roast. And when it was done some big boys came and ran away with it. Then I took the skin and boiled it, drank the soup, and ate the skin, and it was a good supper.

The next day we had nothing to eat but some bark from trees. Later we had a terrible cold spell; the wind drifted so much I knew I would die. The wind blew the tent down. They all crawled out but me. The snow fell on it. I went to sleep and slept warm all night. In the morning I heard someone say, "How many are dead in this tent?" My sister said, "Well, my little brother must be frozen to death in that tent." So they jerked the tent loose, sent it scurrying over the snow. My hair was frozen to the tent. I picked myself up and came out quite alive, to their surprise.

That day we got word that some teams were coming to meet us from the Valley. Three teams came that night. No one but a person having gone through what we had suffered can imagine what a happy moment it was for this "belated handcart company." Men, women, and children knelt down and thanked the Almighty God for our delivery from certain death. It put new life into all the Saints. The next day several more teams arrived, and there was room for all to ride.

We finally arrived in Salt Lake City, November 30, 1856. Our teamster took us to his sister's place, where we were kindly treated. The next day we drove as far as Farmington, Utah, and we stopped at another place that night, and, oh, the difference in treatment. After the grown folks were through eating, there wasn't any food left, and we children were put to bed hungry. Yes, we were half starved. My little sister Maggie and me cried ourselves to sleep. All my life I have worried for fear my children might get as hungry as I was, but thank goodness they have never wanted for food.

❧

Peter Howard McBride's family settled in Ogden City, and later Eden, Weber County, Utah. He married Ruth Burns in 1874, and they became the parents of fourteen children. He also married Laura Lewis in 1882, and they had eight children. Peter was very musically talented—he sang, composed humorous songs, and played numerous instruments. He was called by President Brigham Young to "help promote music and singing" in their area. This "mission" lasted throughout his lifetime. Peter and his family lived the United

Order along the Little Colorado River in Arizona. They later moved to Gila Valley, in Arizona, where they had a 160-acre farm. Peter taught vocal classes at the St. Joseph Academy in Thatcher and served in the bishopric for twenty years. He died April 8, 1932, in Glenbar, Graham County, Arizona.

Sources: Peter Howard McBride. Life Sketch, typescript. In possession of Ella Cochran Madsen, Placerville, California. Original writings in private possession of descendants.

See also *Our Pioneer Heritage,* compiled by Kate B. Carter, 13:359–63. 20 vols. Salt Lake City: Daughters of Utah Pioners, 1970.

MARY ANN STUCKI (HAFEN)

Born: May 5, 1854, Biglen, Bern, Switzerland
Parents: Samuel and Magdalena Stettler Stucki
1860: Oscar O. Stoddard Handcart Company
Age at time of journey: 6

On the shore of the North Sea in Holland, we boarded a small ship. We went down to a large room under the deck. The floor was covered with a thick layer of straw, which came in handy as the sea was very rough. It tossed us about until nearly everyone was sick. I remember Mother sitting on the floor with her back against the wall, holding the baby and trying to brace herself.

After a day and a night's travel we landed at Liverpool, England, or thereabouts. As we walked toward the big sailing ship awaiting us, we were warned by the Mormon elders not to let any stranger carry our bags or children as some had been stolen and sold. I remember how frightened I was when a lady came to my mother and offered to help with her baby. Here we were joined by a large company of emigrants from many countries. There must have been several hundred. As we went on board, we were each vaccinated.

When we set sail, Uncle John Stucki had to stay behind, as he was sick with smallpox. For weeks we were on the Atlantic Ocean. As we children played around, sometimes we stood and watched the cooks kill chickens by wringing their necks. This seemed horrible to me. But afterwards I remember how good the chicken bones tasted that we picked up after the sailors had thrown them away. I remember with pleasure the evening meetings where we enjoyed the sermons of the elders and listened to the Mormon hymns, which I loved even as a child.

One afternoon while we were playing on the deck, one of the sailors pointed out a mermaid. I looked but could see only what seemed to be a lady's head above the water. The sailors told how mermaids would come up to comb their hair and look into a mirror. They said it was a sure sign of storm.

Sure enough there arose a great storm next day. The waves came up like mountains and broke over the deck. We were all ordered under deck, and the water splashed on us as we went down the steps. All night the storm raged. Our ship tossed about like a barrel on a wild sea. Two large beams or masts broke off, and we were driven many miles back.

We were so frightened that we did not go to bed but stayed in a group with the elders praying for safety. Though the captain cried out, "We are lost!" we did not give up hope. We had been promised a safe voyage. The next morning the sun came up bright and clear. We all gave thanks to God for our deliverance. The ship was repaired, and we had pleasant sailing the rest of the way.

At last we saw the lights of New York City. How the people did shout and toss their hats in the air for joy! I remember best my first meal on shore, because we were served with good light bread and sweet milk. After long weeks of *zwieback,* or hard tack, and dried pea soup, this was a happy change.

On our trip to the Missouri River by train, I remember that Brother Wittwer had an accordion and harmonica to help pass the time.

When we reached Florence, Nebraska, near present-day Omaha, we were forced to stop for a while because there were not teams enough to take us across the plains to Salt Lake City. The men set to work making handcarts, and my father, being a carpenter, helped to make thirty-three of them. Ours was a small two-wheeled vehicle with two shafts and a cover on top. The carts were very much like those the street sweepers use in the cities today, except that ours was made entirely of wood, without even an iron rim.

When we came to load up our belongings, we found that we had more than we could take. Mother was forced to leave behind her feather bed, the bolt of linen, two large trunks full of clothes, and some other valuable things which we needed so badly later. Father could take only his most necessary tools.

Our company was organized with Oscar O. Stoddard as captain. It contained 126 persons, with twenty-two handcarts and three provision wagons drawn by oxen. We set out from Florence, Nebraska, on July 6, 1860, for our thousand-mile trip. There were six to our cart. Father and Mother pulled it; Rosie (two years old) and Christian (six months old) rode; John (nine) and I (six) walked. Sometimes, when it was downhill, they let me ride too.

The first night out the mosquitoes gave us a hearty welcome. Father had bought a cow to take along, so we could have milk on the way. At first he tied her to the back of the cart, but she would sometimes hang back, so he thought he would make a harness and have her pull the cart while he led her. By this time Mother's feet were so swollen that she could not wear shoes, but had to wrap her feet with cloth. Father thought that by having the cow pull the cart, Mother might ride. This worked well for some time.

One day a group of Indians came riding up on horses. Their jingling trinkets, dragging poles, and strange appearance frightened the cow and sent her chasing off with the cart and the small children. We were afraid that the children might be killed, but the cow fell into a deep gully, and the cart turned upside down. Although the children were under the trunk and bedding, they were unhurt. But after that, Father did not hitch the cow to the cart again. He let three Danish boys take her to hitch to their cart. Then the Danish boys, each in turn, would help Father pull our cart.

After about three weeks my mother's feet became better so she could wear her shoes again. She would get so discouraged and down-hearted; but father never lost courage. He would always cheer her up by telling her that we were going to Zion, that the Lord would take care of us, and that better times were coming.

Even when it rained, the company did not stop traveling. A cover on the handcart shielded the two younger children. The rest of us found it more comfortable moving than standing still in the drizzle. In fording streams the men often carried the children and weaker women across on their backs. The company stopped over on Sundays for rest, and meetings were held for spiritual comfort and guidance. At night, when the handcarts were drawn up in a circle and the fires were lighted, the camp looked quite happy. Singing, music, and speeches by the leaders cheered everyone. I remember that we stopped one night at an old Indian campground. There were many bright-colored beads in the ant hills.

At times we met or were passed by the overland stagecoach with its passengers and mailbags and drawn by four fine horses. When the Pony Express dashed past, it seemed almost like the wind racing over the prairie.

At last, when we reached the top of Emigration Canyon, overlooking Salt Lake, on that September day, 1860, the whole company stopped to look down through the valley. Some yelled and tossed their hats in the air. A shout of joy arose at the thought that our long trip was over, that we had at last reached Zion, the place of rest. We all gave thanks to God for helping us safely over the plains and mountains to our destination.

❧

In 1861, Mary Ann Stucki settled with her parents and other Swiss Saints in Santa Clara, in Southern Utah. She married Johannes Reber, who died shortly after their marriage. In 1873, she married John George Hafen, the bishop of the Santa Clara Ward, 1884–1912. The couple had eight children. Because of tensions in Utah concerning plural marriage (Mary Ann's husband had other wives), she reared her family in Bunkerville, Nevada. She and her children were among the first settlers there. She was very resourceful, bringing up her children with very little means. She died January 16, 1946, in St. George, Washington County, Utah.

SOURCE: Mary Ann Hafen. *Recollections of a Handcart Pioneer of 1860: With Some Account of Frontier Life in Utah and Nevada*, 18–26. Denver: privately printed, 1938.

JOHN STETTLER STUCKI

Born: December 13, 1850, Heirstetten, Bern, Switzerland
Parents: Samuel and Magdalena Stettler Stucki
1860: Oscar O. Stoddard Handcart Company
Age at time of journey: 9

My dear mother had a little baby to nurse, and only having half enough to eat and to pull on the handcart all day long, day after day, she soon got so weak and worn out that she could not help Father anymore. Nor was she able to keep up with the Company. Sometimes when we camped, she was so far behind the Company we could not see anything of her for quite a while, so that I was afraid she might not be able to get to the camp.

I have never forgotten how when I, a nine-year-old boy, would be so tired that I would wish I could sit down for just a few minutes. How much good it would do to me. But instead of that, my dear, nearly worn-out father would ask me if I could not push a little more on the handcart.

When one of the teamsters, seeing two buffaloes near the oxen, shot one of them, the meat was divided among the whole handcart company. My parents also got a small piece, which my father put in the back end of the handcart. That was in the fore part of the week. Father said we would save it for our dinner next Sunday. I was so very hungry all the time, and the meat smelled so good to me while pushing at the handcart, and having a little pocketknife, I could not resist but had to cut off a piece or two each half day. Although I was afraid of getting a severe whipping after cutting a little the first few times, I could not resist taking a little each half day. I would chew it so long it got tasteless.

When father went to get the meat on Sunday noon, he asked me if I had been cutting off some of it. I said, "Yes, I was so hungry that I could not let it alone." Then, instead of giving me the severe scolding or whipping, he did not say a word but started to wipe the tears from his eyes.

❧

The Stucki family settled with other Swiss Saints in Santa Clara, Utah, in 1861. As a young boy, John helped build the St. George Temple. He married Barbara Baumann, Karolina Heimberg, and Louise Reichenbach. John was the father of twenty-four children, eight of whom were adopted. He was called on a mission to Switzerland, where he served as conference president. After returning home, he taught religion classes. John died March 26, 1933, in Santa Clara, Washington County, Utah.

SOURCE: *Family History Journal of John S. Stucki*, 7, 18–21, 40–46. Salt Lake City: Pyramid Press, 1932. A typescript of the original journal is in the Harold B. Lee Library, Brigham Young University, Provo, Utah.

AGNES CALDWELL (SOUTHWORTH)

Born: February 22, 1847, Glasgow, Lanark, Scotland
Parents: William and Margaret Ann McFall Caldwell
1856: James G. Willie Handcart Company
Age at time of journey: 9

On the twenty-eighth day of June, 1856, under the company leader of James G. Willie, we landed in the United States of America. Then began the noted tramp across the desert waste. Mother had one boy fifteen years of age, upon whom she was depending for the greater share of the pulling; when only a day or two out he was attempting to lasso a wild cow to be milked, his foot became tangled in the rope. He was thrown on his shoulder and dragged quite a distance, sustaining a broken shoulder. This of course threw the heavy pulling upon Mother.

Although only tender years of age, I can yet close my eyes and see everything in panoramic precision before me—the ceaseless walking, walking, ever to remain in my memory. Many times I would become so tired and, childlike, would hang on the cart, only to be gently pushed away. Then I would throw myself by the side of the road and cry. Then realizing they were all passing me by, I would jump to my feet and make an extra run to catch up.

Of the long cold journey, the suffering, and hardships, enough has been told and written, of that terrible night when fifteen were frozen and buried in one grave. My sister Elizabeth Caldwell had her foot frozen. Two of her toes were amputated upon our arrival in the Salt Lake Valley.

I have often marveled of the wonderful integrity of character of my mother's planning and successfully completing such a journey where more able-bodied and stronger—yes, even men—failed miserably.

Winter came in October with eighteen inches of snow, but in spite of this we did not suffer from hunger, due to Mother's careful and frugal planning. In Iowa City Mother sold a quilt and a bedspread for the sum of twenty-four cents. With this she bought food. She had a way with Indians: she traded trinkets for dried meat, which proved to be of great help to us on the journey. Frequently it would be stormy so that a fire could not be built; then mother would allow each of us to have a piece of dried meat on a piece of bread. As food became more and more scarce and the weather colder, she would stew a little of this meat and make a delicious gravy over it. I guess the reason it tasted so good is that we were allowed only a small portion at each meal.

One very cold night, some young men were on guard. Mother prepared some meat broth, thickened with flour, and a little salt; she gave each one of the young men a half pint. They often declared it saved their lives and never before or since had anything tasted so good.

For baking, Mother dug a hole in the ground. The food was placed in a heavy iron kettle with a tight lid on, then set in the hole and covered over with buffalo chips, which were set afire. This produced a nice, even heat, baking the food evenly.

One day we came to a section inhabited by rattlesnakes. Two of us, my friend Mary Hurren and I, would hold hands and jump. It seemed to me we were jumping for more than a mile. Due to the protecting hand of the Lord, we were not harmed.

The 30th of September we stopped at a station in Laramie, Wyoming. Mother, in company with her fifteen-year-old boy and a young lady, Christena McNeil, who was making the trip under Mother's care, visited one of the generals in command at the fort to obtain permission to trade some trinkets and silver spoons for flour and meat. The officer said he himself could not use any of the things but to leave the young lady in his office while mother went to another station, where he assured her she would be able to obtain the things she desired. He seemed very kind, and not wishing to arouse any feeling of ill will, she left Christena and Thomas. During her absence the officer used the time in trying to persuade Christena to stay there, proposing to her and showing her the gold he had, telling her what a fine lady he would make of her. Then he tried discouraging her, pointing out to her how the handcart company would never reach Utah, because of the severe cold, and that they would die of cold and hunger and exposure. Like all noble girls, and true to the cause for which she had left her native Scotland, her family, home, and friends just to be in Utah, she told him in plain language she would take her chances with the others even though it might mean death. She was greatly relieved to have Mother return. The officer, however, seemed to admire her very much for her loyalty to her faith and gave her a large cured ham and wished her well in her chosen adventure.

Just before we crossed the mountains, relief wagons reached us, and it certainly was a relief. The infirm and aged were allowed to ride, all able-bodied continuing to walk. When the wagons started out, a number of us children decided to see how long we could keep up with the wagons, in hopes of being asked to ride. At least that is what my great hope was. One by one they all fell out, until I was the last one remaining, so determined was I that I should get a ride. After what seemed the longest run I ever made before or since, the driver, who was Heber [William Henry] Kimball, called to me, "Say, sissy, would you like a ride?" I answered in my very best manner, "Yes sir." At this he reached over, taking my hand, clucking to his horses to make me run, with legs that seemed to me could run no farther. On we went, to what to me seemed miles. What went through my head at that time was that he was the meanest man that ever lived or that I had ever heard of, and other things that would not be a credit nor would it look well coming from one so young. Just at what seemed the breaking point, he stopped. Taking a blanket, he wrapped me up and lay me in the bottom of the wagon, warm and comfortable. Here I had time to change my mind, as I surely did, knowing full well by doing this he saved me from freezing when taken into the wagon.

∽

Agnes Caldwell and her family arrived safely in the Great Salt Lake Valley November 9, 1856. They settled in Brigham City, Utah, where Agnes met and married Chester Southworth. They became the parents of thirteen children. They lived in Dingle, Idaho, helped settle an LDS colony in Cardston, Alberta, Canada, and lived a short time in Gridley, California, where her husband died in 1910. Agnes moved back to Brigham City for her remaining years, where she was active in Relief Society and enjoyed sewing, quilting, and living close to some of her children. She was an excellent cook and made many Scottish recipes. She died September 11, 1924, in Brigham City at the age of seventy-seven.

SOURCE: "Autobiography of Agnes Caldwell," typescript of interview conducted by Veara Southworth Fife, her daughter. Original in files of Daughters of Utah Pioneers Museum in Salt Lake City, Utah.

Elizabeth White (Stewart)

Born: February 22, 1838, Bloomsbury Square, London, England
Parents: William and Mary Ann Syer White
1856: John A. Hunt Company (This wagon train
traveled alongside the Martin handcart company.)
Age at time of journey: 18

In the above photograph, Elizabeth White Stewart is seated on her horse, Old Birch. On May 22, 1856, Elizabeth left London with her mother, brother Barnard, and sister Eliza. They sailed from Liverpool to the Boston Harbor and then traveled by train twelve hundred miles to Iowa City, Iowa.

When we completed our journey to Iowa City, we were informed that we would have to walk four miles to our camping ground. All felt delighted to have the privilege of a pleasant walk. We all started, about five hundred of us, with our bedding. We had not gone far before it began to thunder and lightning, and the rain poured. The roads became very muddy and slippery. The day was far advanced, and it was late in the evening before we arrived at the camp. We all got very wet. The boys soon got our tent up, so we were fixed for the night, although very wet. We camped there until September.

We had about forty wagons in our company, led by Captain John Hunt. We got along real well, had no trouble with Indians, but when we were near Fort Laramie, Wyoming, a herd of buffalos came along as we were traveling and caused our cattle to stampede, resulting in the death of Mrs. Walters. She was driving the team in front of ours. She was knocked down and trampled upon by the oxen. She never spoke, but died in a few minutes, leaving a young baby. This sad affair cast a gloom over our camp. She was sewed in a blanket and buried on the wayside.

The weather was fair, and we got along real well until we were near the Platte River. It was getting very cold by this time. We finally reached the last crossing of the Platte River. We were then about five hundred miles from Salt Lake. Our company camped on the east side, and the handcart company passed over that night. All our able-bodied men turned out to help them carry women and children over the river. Some of our men went through the river seventy-five times. The snow fell six inches during that night; there were thirteen deaths during the night. They were so worn out. This was on the twentieth of October.

By the time we reached Devil's Gate, in Wyoming, we were nearly out of provisions. Our dear mother said she had never seen her dear family want for bread, but said the Lord would provide. About midnight that night all the camp had retired, and we were awakened with a noise and thought it was the yelling of Indians. We got up expecting they were upon us, but to our great surprise the noise was caused by the teamsters of a relief team, and some of the camp shouted for joy. They were loaded with all kinds of provisions: flour, bread, butter, meat of all kinds, but all frozen so hard. Everything was so good. The bread was like cake, so sweet and nice. I remember we had to cut everything with the hatchet, but oh how thankful we all were that the Lord had answered our prayers and saved us all from starvation. Through the timely action of President

Brigham Young in organizing this company, we were saved. The loaded wagon that came to our camp was from Draper, Utah. George Clawson and Gurnsey Brown were the teamsters.

When we got to the foot of the big mountain, the snow was so deep I had to put men's boots on. The teamsters were tall, and so was Esther Brown, and she could step in their tracks, but I could not in hers, and I had to make my own road up both mountains, frequently falling down. The snow was so deep and drifted, but they told us when we got to the top we would see Salt Lake City. We were so thankful and delighted that it seemed to renew our strength and energy. It was the hardest part of my journey, but the thought of being nearly at our journey's end after six months traveling and camping was cheering.

When we got to the top of the big mountains, the men folks took off their hats, and we waved our handkerchiefs. They then pointed out Salt Lake City, and I could not believe it was, for it looked to me like a patch of sagebrush covered with snow. I could not believe it until we got nearly to it. We arrived in Salt Lake City just at sundown on the thirtieth day of November 1856.

❦

Elizabeth White married Isaac Mitton Stewart in 1857, and they became the parents of eleven children. They lived in Draper, Utah, where her husband was a well-known educator and a bishop. While rearing her family, Elizabeth milked cows, made all their butter and soap, and wove the cloth from which she sewed her children's clothing. In her later years, Elizabeth said, "I have knitted for my great-grandchildren over sixty pairs of stockings. I am seventy-eight years old and still doing my own work." Elizabeth died May 7, 1917, in Salt Lake City.

Source: "Autobiography of Elizabeth White Stewart," typescript. In *Ancestors of Isaac Mitton Stewart and Elizabeth White*, compiled by Mary Ellen B. Workman. Privately printed, 1978.

Robert Reeder

Born: May 24, 1837, Linstead, Suffolk, England
Parents: David and Lydia Balls Reeder
1856: James G. Willie Handcart Company
Age at time of journey: 19

On the 5th of May we sailed out from Liverpool, England, on the great ocean, which took us a little over six weeks to cross. I was very sick on the way and could not eat such food as they had on "seafare," which consisted of what they called sea biscuits and salt pork and salt beef, also brown sugar and vinegar and very little other food. I got very feeble living principally on sugar and vinegar for three weeks.

I was glad when we arrived at Castle Garden, New York, where we could get a piece of bread once more. We rested here a few days, then pursued our journey by railroad and steamboats, changing from one to the other until we arrived at the Iowa camping ground, where we had to lay over two or three weeks waiting for our outfits.

While laying over there, we had to herd those cattle night and day. There were lots of us to change off if all would have taken a part, but it was a very rainy country, and some would not take their turn, especially in the nighttime. I can well remember those who had charge used to come to us and say, "Will you go and herd again tonight as we cannot get anyone else to go." Me and my father and my brother-in-law, James Hurren, have gone three and four nights out of a week in the pouring rain, wet through from head to foot and in the water part of the time up to our knees—anything to help get fitted out and started on the road.

When our handcart company got out about three hundred miles on the road, our cattle stampeded, most all of our best oxen leaving, which left us in a bad state to move any farther. We stayed there for several days, hunting as far as we dared to go to find some of our cattle but could not find any, believing the Indians must have driven them away. Then some of the flour was taken out of the wagons and put on the handcarts according to the strength of the party drawing them. Some had one, others two or three, and, if my memory serves me right, Brother Hurren, being considered the strongest man the company had, had five sacks put on his cart besides two small girls that were not able to walk and all his baggage and cooking utensils. His wife helped in pulling the cart and walked the entire trial.

My father, David Reeder, would start out in the morning and pull his cart until he would drop on the road. He did this day after day until he did not arise early on October 7, 1856. He was found dead in his bed, and his fellow bedmate had not heard a thing during the night. Sister Eliza wrapped a cherished sheet around him, and we placed him in a shallow grave, hoping the wolves would not disturb. We must go on our way in silent mourning and in a weakened condition.

Our rations were growing shorter, and we reduced them by common consent from day to day. Nights were getting colder, and some would sit down by the roadside and die. My younger sister, Caroline, seventeen years old, after traveling all day and seeing the camp being made for the night, took off her apron to tie some sagebrush in to bring into the camp. She sat down to rest, leaning on her bundle, exhausted. They found her chilled and dying and carried her to camp. She died without gaining consciousness. She, too, was placed in an unmarked grave near Three Crossings—Sweetwater River. She died the evening of October 15, 1856. Her death was another real loss to us, but we must hurry on in threatening weather and colder nights on the Windriver Pass. So it was with others, as many as thirteen being buried in one grave at one time. I think fully one hundred died on this trip.

On October 17, we awoke covered with eight inches of snow and rations about gone. We pulled our carts sixteen miles in a blinding snow storm and arrived at Rock Creek, where we sheltered against the hill as best we could to avoid the north wind and blowing snow. Weakened to such an extent and without food, thirteen died that night. All the able-bodied men dug one large grave, but not too deep. My brother-in-law, James Hurren, held out his eight-year-old girl Mary to see her little playmate lying among the dead. They were laid away in the clothes they wore, in a circle with feet to center and heads out. We covered them with willows and then earth and slid rocks down the hill to keep the wolves from disturbing them. Two of the men who helped dig the grave died and were buried in another nearby. We could go no further. The weather was severe, and we had not a morsel of food in camp. We had heard assistance was on the road, and we still had hopes.

When the relief party heard of our terrible situation, they doubled up teams and came to us as quickly as possible. They reached us after we had been in camp forty-eight hours. They dared not give us much food for fear of killing us all.

Through snow and wind we mostly walked behind the relief wagons about three hundred miles to Salt Lake City and arrived on Public Square [where the Joseph Smith Memorial Building now stands] November 9, 1856. We stopped for about two hours, and many of the Church authorities came and talked to us. Then we were given over to the bishops of the different wards. Each bishop took a few, whom they saw got some kind of work to pay for their keep during the winter.

❧

Robert Reeder made two trips back to the Missouri River to help emigrants on their way to Utah. While on the first trip he found the grave of his father, David Reeder. Robert married Lydia Wilkinson in 1861, and they were among the earliest settlers in Hyde Park, Cache County, Utah. They became the parents of five children. He later married Ellen Flatt, and they had nine children. He was a cattle man, butcher, deputy sheriff, and hay merchant. Robert Reeder died December 22, 1917, and he is buried in the Hyde Park Cemetery.

SOURCES: Robert Reeder. Autobiography, typescript, in possession of granddaughter, Doris Reeder, Hyde Park, Utah. The original is in the Daughters of Utah Pioneers Museum in Salt Lake City.

See also *Heart Throbs of the West,* compiled by Kate B. Carter, 2:187. 12 vols. Salt Lake City: Daughters of Utah Pioneers, 1940.

Part Four

NARROW ESCAPES

"My flesh and my heart faileth: but God is the strength of my heart, and my portion for ever."

∽ PSALM 73:26

Many Mormon pioneers had frightening experiences while crossing the Great Plains. Young pioneers typically worried about encountering hostile Indians or wild animals or becoming lost. These concerns were often reinforced by parents who warned their children daily to stay close to the company and huddle near the wagon or an adult whenever a Pawnee or Sioux approached.

Morning and evening prayers were filled with pleas to God to protect and shield the travelers from the dangers they faced. The way young pioneers and their parents responded to their close calls is another measure of their faith and courage.

Edwin Alfred Pettit

Born: February 16, 1834, Hempstead, Queens, New York
Parents: Jesse and Mary Pettit Pettit*
1847: Edward Hunter Company
Age at time of journey: 13

Edwin's mother's maiden name was also Pettit.

While the Pettit family was living in Nauvoo, Illinois, the parents died within two weeks of each other in 1842, leaving Edwin and his siblings to be cared for by a court-appointed guardian.

In February, 1846, the people began leaving Nauvoo for the West, and my sister and her husband decided to go with them. I was given to understand that if I wished to go West, there would be a way provided for me. I wanted to go with my sister, but the rest of the children opposed my going, as did also my guardian.

A man was sent from the Mormon camp to pilot me to the camp of my sister, which was some miles away. This young man took me to the camp; but my guardian and brothers followed me and took me back on horseback. I didn't get to see my sister as they overtook me before I reached her.

In a short time there was another man who made his appearance in the neighborhood on the same errand, a man that I was acquainted with. We made an appointment to meet at a certain place and make our escape if possible. I got up very early in the morning and went downstairs with my shoes in my hands. My guardian was dozing in his chair as I slipped out unknown to him, and put my shoes on outside. I soon fell in with my friend, and we tramped all day without anything to eat to reach the spot where I was to join my sister. Instead of going into camp, I lay out in the prairie all night alone. The captain of this company called the people together and told them if there was anybody inquiring for a boy to tell them there was no such boy in camp—I was not in the camp at this time; I was staying out in the prairie. The parties came hunting for me again but failed to find me.

Disguised as a girl, and in company with four or five girls, I crossed the Des Moines River on a flat boat, the boatman being none the wiser, supposing I was a girl with the rest. I was wearing side combs in my hair, and false curls covered my head. I was also wearing a sunbonnet in order to make my disguise more complete.

On landing on the opposite side of the river, I met an old friend on horseback, and he took me on behind him. As is well-known, girls are supposed to ride sidewise, especially where there are a great many people to observe them, and I also took that precaution. In going along the road, the people would sometimes holler out, "Old man, that girl will fall—she's asleep," because I was trying to hide my face. He turned around and said, "Mary Ann, wake up. You'll fall off and break your neck." I at last reached my sister's camp, near a place called Indian Creek.

In the spring of 1847 we moved camp and passed through Winter Quarters, where the main part of the Saints had been camped all winter. All the companies were organized into companies of hundreds, fifties, and tens, with a captain over each.

Fuel was very scarce most of the time, and when we wanted a fire, everyone would go out to gather buffalo chips, and some of the daintier sex, instead of picking them up with their hands, used tongs to gather them with. Before we had gone very far, they got very bravely over this, and would almost fight over a dry one. We could see buffalo as thick as the leaves on the trees for miles around. We had a great deal of trouble from the buffalo, having to scare them away with guns in order to make a passage.

In the latter part of the journey, when our cattle began to get tired and footsore, sometimes lying down, it was a difficult matter to get them on their feet again.

After a journey of about four or five months, we reached Salt Lake on the 29th day of September, 1847. We joined some of the immigrants on what is now known as Pioneer Square. It was then surrounded by a high mud wall as a protection against the Indians, with portholes on all sides and a large gate on each side. I lived near the northwest corner of the square, where my brother-in-law and sister and myself had two houses of one room each. Many a time we have stood with an umbrella over the table to keep the water from coming through on our food, and tin pans set over the bed to catch the water that dripped through the mud roof.

Edwin Pettit was heavily involved in freighting and in helping immigrants coming to Utah from California, where he had settled in 1851. While assisting others, he crossed the Nevada desert seventeen times by team and three times by rail. He married Maria Pettit Bush, a widow with two sons, and they had one daughter. After her death, he married Rebecca Hood Hill, and they became the parents of fourteen children. Edwin died April 17, 1924, in Salt Lake City, Utah.

SOURCE: Edwin Pettit. *Biography of Edwin Pettit 1834–1912*, 6–10. Salt Lake City: The Arrow Press, 1912.

GEORGE SUDBURY HUMPHERYS

Born: April 19, 1842, Nottingham, Nottinghamshire, England
Parents: Thomas and Mary Sudbury Humpherys
1861: James Clayton Wagon Train
Age at time of journey: 19

In the above photograph, George Humpherys is seated at center, surrounded by his brothers and sisters.

I was talking to the assistant wagon master and driving the lead team, when we heard a terrible yell. We looked up the road and saw a large band of Indians coming towards us.

They were very modest in their request, for they demanded 10 yoke of oxen, 1000 lbs. of flour, 300 lbs. sugar, 100 lbs. coffee, and 100 lbs. bacon. If we wouldn't give it to them, we would have to fight and they would take what they wanted. There was between three and four hundred Indians. Some of the men wanted to fight it out with them, but our wagon master, Mr. James Clayton, would not hear of that if there was any other way to get along with them. He told us to prepare for the worst, for we may have to fight, but he would do all he could to avoid it.

After talking to them for some time, he thought of the man in our group with smallpox. He told the chief to go with him to the wagon where the sick man lay. A number of the Indians followed their chief, thinking they were going to get all they asked for.

But when they got within twenty-five yards of the wagon, Mr. Clayton called to the sick man to look out of the wagon for he wanted to see him. He arose and looked out. The scales were just falling off his face. The chief gave a look and said, "Smallpox!" He turned his horse and yelled for his men to follow, and they did so. It was almost two miles to the Platte River, and they rode as fast as they could till they got there. Then they crossed and looked around for a few minutes, then rode off again. Mr. Clayton was watching them through a large glass.

We could not get sight of an Indian for three weeks after that. We had to conclude that smallpox was a very good thing to have close by.

❧

George Humpherys, who came to Utah in 1856, served a mission to Great Britain, 1896–98. He married Sarah Ann Eaton in 1864, and they had ten children. They lived in Paris, Idaho, where he was known to be friendly, to have a clever wit, and to be an excellent gardener. He died May 19, 1922, at the age of eighty.

Source: George Humpherys. Autobiographical sketch, holograph. LDS Church Archives.

FANNY FRY (SIMONS)

Born: September 6, 1842, Portsmouth, Hampshire, England
Parents: John James and Ann Toomer Fry
1859: George Rowley Company
Age at time of journey: 16

Fanny left England with her brother, John, and her sister, Sarah. Their father had disappeared at sea and was presumed dead, and their mother remained in England another five years before joining them in Utah. Fanny describes her feelings as her mother helped her pack for the journey:

I could not describe my feelings while these preparations were going on. It seemed that I was in a complete daze or dream from which I expected to awaken and find it all a delusion. My feelings at this time can better be imagined than described. Mother had her photograph picture taken and gave one to each of us, and it was a prize to me, for it was five long years before I saw her again.

The three young people safely crossed the ocean on the ship the William Tapscott. *Fanny describes one incident:*

We had one slight storm lasting only six hours, just strong enough to rock the boat nicely. I remember Jimmie Bond, for he was such a jolly fellow. His wife was lying sick in her berth; he was kneeling at an unlashed trunk when the ship began to rock. It pushed him under the berth and back again in quick succession, and he was singing all the while, "Here we go, there we go again," the trunk following him each time. It was quite laughable to those looking on, but not, I suppose, for Jimmie.

Fanny's brother, John, remained in New York for a short time to work, and Fanny and her sister traveled to Florence, Nebraska. Fanny joined a handcart company while her sister, Sarah, traveled with another company.

Well, we started from Florence, Nebraska, on the seventh of June. That memorable day I shall never forget in this life. We traveled three miles the first day. Brother Coltrin pulled the cart in my place, and I walked beside him. He felt so sorry for us because he knew what was before us and we knew nothing of it, he having just made the journey.

There were fifty-eight handcarts, with an average of three to a cart. Our rations when we started was a pint of flour a day, and we had some bacon and soap. These items soon gave out. We had to take a cold water wash for the want of a vessel to warm the water in. And not having soap, we were worse than ever.

At the Elk Horn River, my feet were so swollen I could not wear my shoes. Then when the swelling went out, my feet were so sore from the alkali that I never had on a pair of shoes after that for the entire journey.

After a while we recovered our usual spirits and enjoyed ourselves evenings around camp visiting each other, with singing and other amusements. There was one song we would sing which would make the shivers creep over me:

Do they miss me at home? Do they miss me?
It would be an assurance most dear
To know at this moment some loved one
Were saying, "I wish he was here,"
To know that the group near the fireside
Were thinking of me as I roam.
Oh, it would be joy beyond measure
To know that they missed me at home.

I recollect one day the captain put me to a cart with six people's luggage on and only three to pull it—a woman, a lad of sixteen, and I, seventeen—and there was nine days' bread. All grown people were allowed twenty pounds of luggage apiece and their cooking utensils besides. That made quite a load for us. I know it was the hardest day's work I ever remember doing in all my life before or since. We had to pull up quite a long hill, and part of it was steep. In climbing we got behind one of the teams for the oxen to help us, for it was all we could do to keep it moving. Captain Rowley came up and called us lazy, and that I did not consider we were at all.

While pulling this heavy load, I looked and acted strange. The first thing my friend Emmie knew I had fallen under the cart, and before they could stop it, the cart had passed over me, and I lay at the back of it on the ground.

When my companions got to me, I seemed perfectly dead. Emmie could not find any pulse at all, and there was not a soul around. They were, she thought, all ahead, so she stood thinking what to do when Captain Rowley came up to us. "What have you got there, Emmie?" he said. "Oh my, Fanny is dead," she said. It frightened him, so he got off his horse and examined me closely but could not find any life at all. He asked Emmie to stay with me and he would go and stop the company and send a cart back for me, which he did.

When I came to myself, my grave was dug two feet deep, and I was in a tent. The sisters had sewed me up to the waist in my blanket, ready for burial. I opened my eyes and looked at them.

I was weak for some time after. I did not fully recover during the rest of the journey. Through it all I found I had a great many friends in the company.

Soon, the handcart company began running out of food. They made some soup that made everyone ill, and the entire company was in a very desperate condition. They decided to stop and camp until they could obtain more food.

On the morning of the fourth day after camping, one of the brethren related a dream he had that night. He told us that the Church teams would come that day, and just before we could see them we would hear a gun fired and they would come in sight. I think it was in the afternoon that we heard a gun shot, and in a minute the teams came in sight, six in number.

Oh, I will never forget that time, especially the next few minutes; they seem so plain to me even now. I think that some of the faces of the men are stamped on my memory forever. The teams came trotting down the hill. The wagon master decided he would have some fun with us, so he told the boys to shout "Hurrah for Pikes Peak" and then drive on past us. They did so. Oh, how our hearts failed us! We had all got out to the road to meet them and had made an opening in the circle of carts for them to drive in. Men and women threw themselves on the ground, begging for a crust for their last meal. It was a sight that none who witnessed it will ever forget. The wagon master, poor fellow, was melted to tears.

"Boys! he said, "I can't stand this; drive in." They drove in, and then we began to scramble into the wagons. "Stand back, brethren and sisters, until we can get the horses away, and then we will give you all you can eat." The teamster told us when that was gone to come and get more and to eat plenty—that if they had not brought enough they could send to Salt Lake City and get more. We were to have all we could eat, and we did from that time to the end of the journey.

The day we were going over Big Mountain, I was learning to ride horseback, and a nice picture I looked, I can assure you: an old sunbonnet on my head all torn, an old jacket, and my petticoat tattered, and my feet dressed in rags. That was my costume. I was riding in advance of the entire company. I saw a wagon coming towards me; I rode on, and the wagon was passing all right. When about past, I saw some well-dressed ladies sitting in the wagon, and one of them cried, "There goes my sister." The next thing I knew I was in the wagon in my darling sister's arms. Oh the rapture of that moment! It was blessed to me, I will say. Sarah had arrived in Salt Lake City sometime since and got rested, and now Brother and Sister Eddington were coming with her to meet me and the handcart company. They had heard that the company would camp in the canyon that night, and they had come prepared to stay all night with us and fetch some of us. They brought with them a quarter of young beef, half a lamb, pies and cakes that I was to divide among my friends.

❧

Fanny Fry arrived in Salt Lake City, on September 6, 1859. She married John Zundel, and they became the parents of one daughter. After John's death, she married Gustavus Simons, and they had three children. Fanny earned extra income for the family by nursing the sick and weaving carpets. Fanny died December 22, 1916. She is buried in Payson, Utah County, Utah.

Sources: Fanny Fry Simons. Journal, holograph, in possession of her granddaughter, Georgia Hansen, Spanish Fork, Utah.

See also "Journal of Fanny Fry Simons." In *An Enduring Legacy*, 6:178–212. 12 vols. Salt Lake City: Daughters of Utah Pioneers, 1983.

Part Five
SUFFER THE CHILDREN

"He shall feed his flock like a shepherd: he shall gather the lambs
with his arm, and carry them in his bosom, and shall gently lead
those that are with young."

ᴥ ISAIAH 40:11

Between 1847 and the coming of the railroad to Ogden in 1869, several hundred souls died along the Mormon Trail, from exhaustion, exposure, disease, and lack of food. Very few were killed by Indians. Travelers along the trail were subdued as they passed burial mounds along the way, silent witnesses of the suffering and death of some of those ahead of them. By the banks of streams, on grassy knolls, in the sands, beneath groves of trees, or among piles of rock, the graves were dug.

Many of those who lost their lives were children and the elderly, those least able to fight off the effects of disease and the harsh elements. Their deaths were every bit as tragic as those young mothers and fathers who succumbed to the dangers and illnesses associated with the American frontier. They left behind grieving children, including some too young to understand a loss that would change their lives forever.

If narrow escapes are the raw material of high adventure, these stories of those who sacrificed their lives or suffered because of the deaths of their loved ones are the stuff of tragic and inspiring heroism.

PETER WESTON MAUGHAN,
Story Told by His Mother

Peter Weston Maughan
Born: May 20, 1847, New Diggins, Lafayette County, Wisconsin
Parents: Peter and Mary Ann Weston Maughan
1850: Warren Foote Company
Age at time of journey: 3

Above portrait is of Peter's mother, Mary Ann Weston Maughan. The following incident, as told by Peter's mother, took place just west of Fort Kearney, Nebraska:

About noon as we were traveling along on a good plain road, my little Peter, about three years old, was sitting in the front of the wagon between his brother Charles and his sister Mary Ann. They were looking at a cow that had lost one horn. He leaned forward, lost his balance, and fell before the wheels. The first passed over him, and he tried to escape the other one. But alas, the wagon stopped just as the hind wheel stood on his dear little back. The brethren from behind ran up and lifted the wheel and took him from under it. He was bruised internally so that it was impossible for him to live long.

We did all that was possible for him, but no earthly power could save him. He did not suffer much pain. The people left their wagons and gathered around mine, and all wept for the dear little boy that we knew must soon leave us. I had talked to him many times to be careful and not fall out of the wagon, or he might be hurt very bad.

I did not know that his father had fainted, for the brethren stood to hide him from my sight. On my asking for him, they said he would come soon. As soon as he was able, he came to the wagon, covered with dust. But his little boy could not speak to him. He opened his eyes and looked so lovingly at us, then gently closed them and passed peacefully away and left us weeping around his dear little bruised body.

Then loving hands tenderly dressed him in a suit of his own white linen clothes. He looked so lovely. I emptied a dry goods box, and Brother Wood made him a nice coffin; and it even was a mournful satisfaction, for we had seen our brothers and sisters bury their dear ones without a coffin to lay them in.

We buried him on a little hill on the north side of the road. The grave was consecrated, and then they laid him to rest. Someone had made a nice headboard with his name printed on, also his age and date of death. This was all we could do, and many prayers were offered to our Heavenly Father that he might rest in peace and not be disturbed. We turned away in sorrow and grief.

A few days after, we heard that his grave had not been touched, but another little one made beside it, and afterwards some more were buried by them. This was a great satisfaction to us, to know that he remained as we left him.

❧

Peter Weston Maughan died July 12, 1850. His parents were among the first settlers in Wellsville, Cache County, Utah. Weston, Idaho, was named in honor of his mother.

SOURCES: Mary Ann Weston Maughan. Autobiography, typescript. Special Collections, Merrill Library, Utah State University, Logan, Utah.

See also *Our Pioneer Heritage,* 2:376–77.

CHRISTIAN LYNGAA CHRISTENSEN

Born: April 29, 1855, Nielstrup, Randers, Denmark
Parents: Niels Christian and Karen Nielsen Christensen
1860: Carl Wederberg "Independent" Company
Age at time of journey: 5

My parents embraced Mormonism before I was born. We immigrated to Utah in 1860. We sailed in an old vessel called the *William Tapscott*, an English ship. It had the old style sails. When we landed in the U.S., we rode by train some distance.

Our outfitting place, where we bought oxen, wagons, cows, etc., was at Florence, Nebraska. Our company was presided over by a man called Carl Wederberg, who once had been a Catholic Priest in Norway but by now a very prominent Mormon, our spiritual guide. We had two men from Utah who were our pilots. They had crossed the plains often with other outfits. One was A. H. Pattison of Payson, Utah, the other was Nephi Johnson of Southern Utah. They were both young men, and how they managed such a babble of tongues is more than ordinary mortals can tell. Danes, Swedes, Norwegians, German, and English, and none of them had ever seen an ox team in their lives. It must have been a stupendous undertaking.

We encountered many of the Sioux Indians traveling parallel with us. On the 26th of August, while thus traveling, they stole a Danish maid, thirty-five years old, who was behind the wagon train driving an old lame cow. She had a young lad along to help her. A young, robust warrior took hold of her and carried her off on a white horse. She fought him desperately, so she managed to dismount often, and he had to drag her back again. But it delayed his travel, so the lad had time to run and get some help. The eighty wagons were circled into a corral as usual when we camped, and five men with guns in hand went to the rescue of the stolen woman. When they got back to the cow, the Indian was still in sight. Nephi Johnson, who was an unusual Indian interpreter, got an old Indian to go and bring the woman back, which he did. For this friendly act they gave him the old cow. Father was one of the five men. It was quite a formidable army amongst 1800 Sioux Indians. The woman hid for several days in the wagon under a feather bed. She had been terribly frightened.

On the first of September, 1860, after crossing the North Platte River, we camped for noon on Horse Shoe Creek. Father came up to our wagon, and Mother announced that the pancakes were ready. He answered that he did not care to eat and said to Mother, "I understand there are many sage hens on the creek, and as we have many sick folks in the train, I will go and try for some fresh meat for them." He picked up his double-barreled shotgun and passed over to the East side, where he fell in with S. M. Lovendahl, a Swedish friend.

The two had not been gone long when a shot was heard, and Mr. Lovendahl came running into camp for help. He had shot Father. Nephi Johnson and others grabbed some bedding and ran to the wounded man's assistance. Mother and I got there as they were laying him on some bedding. He said but little, but it was all for the welfare of his widow and two small boys, one 5 1/2 years old and the other 3 1/2, and the prospect of another soon to be. It appears that Mr. Lovendahl had seen some sage hens, and they had dodged out of his sight, and while he yet had his gun cocked, he fell over some obstacle and shot Father in the bowels. About one-half of the shot hit the stock of Father's gun, but enough hit Father so he died sometime during the night.

Next morning before sunrise he was buried by the wayside in an unknown grave. His coffin was burlap sacks; and his gravestone, a buffalo skull. It was wonderful to see the sympathy and pity and weeping for Mother by large, husky women of the Great Sioux Nation, who had befriended us out in the wilderness on the plains of Nebraska.

An old German gentleman took me by the hand, and each day we walked ahead of the train as far as the pilot would let us. We had a chance often to sit down and rest. He provided me with lunch each day, and I never shall forget the many times he would say, "*Du haf ein gut fadder.*" (You have a good father.) I walked all the way from where Father died to Salt Lake City, where we arrived November 23, 1860.

Christian Lyngaa Christensen served as a missionary to the Indians in Arizona for several years. He married Ann Elizabeth Thompson, Severina Jensen, and Ane Johanne Jensen and was the father of twenty children. He knew seven languages, which earned him the nickname of "Chris-lingo." He died November 26, 1940, in Monticello, San Juan County, Utah.

Sources: Typescript of the original records of Christian Lyngaa Christensen. Harold B. Lee Library, Brigham Young University, Provo, Utah, and Utah State Historical Society Library, Salt Lake City.

See also "Leaves from the Journal of C. L. Christensen." In *Heart Throbs of the West*, 9:1–3. 1948.

MARY GOBLE (PAY)

Born: June 2, 1843, Brighton, Sussex, England
Parents: William and Harriet Johnson Goble
1856: John A. Hunt Company
Age at time of journey: 13

When I was in my twelfth year, my parents joined the Latter-day Saints. On the fifth of November I was baptized. The following May we started for Utah. We left our home May 19, 1856. We came to London the first day, the next day came to Liverpool and went on board the ship *Horizon* that eve.

It was a sailing vessel, and there were nearly nine hundred souls on board. We sailed on the 25th. The pilot ship came and tugged us out into the open sea.

I well remember how we watched old England fade from sight. We sang "Farewell Our Native Land, Farewell."

When we were a few days out, a large shark followed the vessel. One of the Saints died, and he was buried at sea. We never saw the shark any more.

When we were sailing through the banks of Newfoundland, we were in a dense fog for several days. The sailors were kept busy night and day, ringing bells and blowing foghorns. One day I was on deck with my father when I saw a mountain of ice in the sea close to the ship. I said, "Look, Father, look." He went as white as a ghost and said, "Oh, my girl." At that moment the fog parted, the sun shone brightly till the ship was out of danger, when the fog closed on us again.

We were on the sea six weeks, then we landed at Boston. We took the train for Iowa City, where we had to get an outfit for the plains. It was the end of July. On the first of August we started to travel, with our ox teams unbroken and we not knowing a thing about driving oxen.

When we were in the Iowa campground, there came up a thunderstorm that blew down our shelter, made with handcarts and some quilts. We sat there in the rain, thunderstorm and lightning. My sister Fanny got wet and died the 19th of July 1856. She would have been 2 years old on the 23rd. [She had broken out with the measles on the ship, and was thus in a weakened position.] The day we started our journey, we visited her grave. We felt very bad to leave our little sister there.

We traveled through the States until we came to Council Bluffs, Iowa. Then we started on our journey of one thousand miles over the plains. It was about the first of September. We traveled fifteen to twenty-five miles a day. We used to stop one day in the week to wash. On Sunday we would hold our meetings and rest. Every morning and night we were called to prayers by the bugle.

The Indians were on the war path and very hostile. Our captain, John Hunt, had us make a dark camp. That was to stop and get our supper, then travel a few miles, and not light any fires but camp and go to bed. The men had to travel all day and guard every other night.

We traveled on till we got to the Platte River. That was the last walk I ever had with my mother. We caught up with handcart companies that day. We watched them cross the river. There were great lumps of ice floating down the river. It was bitter cold. The next morning there were fourteen dead in camp through the cold. We went back to camp and went to prayers. They sang, "Come, Come, Ye Saints, No Toil Nor Labor Fear." I wondered what made my mother cry. That night my mother took sick, and the next morning my little sister was born. It was the 23rd of September. We named her Edith, and she lived six weeks and died for want of nourishment.

We had been without fresh water for several days, just drinking snow water. The captain said there was a spring of fresh water just a few miles away. It was snowing hard, but my mother begged me to go and get her a drink. Another lady went with me. We were about halfway to the spring when we found an old man who had fallen in the snow. He was so stiff we could not lift him, so the lady told me where to go, and I would go back for help, for we knew he would soon be frozen if we left him. When I had gone, I began to think of the Indians and began looking in all directions. I became confused and forgot the way I should go. I waded around in the snow up to my knees and became lost. Later when I did not return to camp, the men started out after me. It was 11:00 o'clock before they found me. My feet and legs were frozen. They carried me to camp and rubbed me with snow. They put my feet in a bucket of water. The pain was terrible. The frost came out of my legs and feet but not out of my toes.

We traveled in the snow from the last crossing of the Platte River. We had orders not to pass the handcart companies. We had to keep close to them so as to help them if we could. We began to get short of food; our cattle gave out. We could only travel a few miles a day. When we started out of camp in the morning, the brethren would shovel snow to make a track for our cattle. They were weak for the want of food as the buffaloes were in large herds by the roads and ate all the grass.

When we arrived at Devil's Gate, it was bitter cold. We left lots of our things there. There were two or three log houses there. We left our wagon and joined teams with a man named James Barman. We stayed there two or three days. While there an ox fell on the ice and the brethren killed it, and the beef was given out to the camp. My brother James ate a hearty supper and was as well as he ever was when he went to bed. In the morning he was dead.

My feet were frozen, also my brother Edwin and my sister Caroline had their feet frozen. It was nothing but snow. We could not drive out the cold in our tents. Father would clean a place for our tents and put snow around to keep it down. We were short of flour, but Father was a good shot. They called him the hunter of the camp. So that helped us out. We could not get enough flour for bread as we got only a quarter of a pound per head a day, so we would make it like thin gruel. We called it "skilly."

There were four companies on the plains. We did not know what would become of us. One night a man came to our camp and told us there would be plenty of flour in the morning, for Brother Young had sent men and teams to help us. There was rejoicing that night. We sang songs, some danced, and some cried.

We traveled faster now that we had horse teams. My mother had never got well; she lingered until the 11th of December, the day we arrived in Salt Lake City, 1856. She died between the Little and Big Mountains. She was buried in the Salt Lake City Cemetery. She was forty-three years old. She and her baby lost their lives gathering to Zion in such a late season of the year. My sister was buried at the last crossing of the Sweetwater River.

We arrived in Salt Lake City at nine o'clock at night the 11th of December 1856. Three out of the four that were living were frozen. My mother was dead in the wagon.

Bishop Hardy had us taken to a house in his ward and the brethren and the sisters brought us plenty of food. We had to be careful and not eat too much as it might kill us we were so hungry.

Early next morning Brother Brigham Young and a doctor came. The doctor's name was Williams. When Brigham Young came in, he shook hands with all of us. When he saw our condition—our feet frozen and our mother dead—tears rolled down his cheeks.

The doctor wanted to cut my feet off at the ankle, but President Young said, "No, just cut off the toes, and I promise you that you will never have to take them off any farther." The doctor amputated my toes, using a saw and a butcher knife. The sisters were dressing mother for her grave. Oh how did we stand it? That afternoon she was buried.

We had been in Salt Lake a week, when one afternoon a knock came at the door. It was Uncle John Wood. When he met Father he said, "I know it all, Bill." Both of them cried. I was glad to see my father cry.

Instead of my feet getting better, they got worse until the following July. I went to Dr. Wiseman's. But it was no use—he could do no more for me unless I would consent to have them cut off at the ankle. I told him what Brigham Young had promised me. He said, "All right, sit there and rot. I will do nothing more until you come to your senses."

One day, I sat there crying, my feet were hurting so, when a little old woman knocked at the door. She said she had felt that someone needed her there. I told her the promise that Brigham Young had made me. She made a poultice and put it on my feet, and every day she would come and change the poultice. At the end of three months my feet were well.

One day Dr. Wiseman said, "Well, Mary, I must say you have grit. I suppose your feet have rotted to the knees by this time." I said, "Oh, no, my feet are well." He said, "I know better, it could never be." So I took off my stockings and showed him my feet. He said that was surely a miracle.

ᕙ

Mary Goble married Richard Pay in 1859, and they made a living ranching in Nephi, Juab County, Utah. She and her husband became the parents of thirteen children, ten sons and three daughters. Mary learned the Indian language so she could communicate with the many Indians who visited their home. The couple frequently gave the natives fruit and chickens to eat. She once drove Chief Blackhawk out of her orchard with sticks and stones because he was picking too many of her peaches. Mary was left a widow in 1893 with nine children still at home. She earned extra income as a midwife and a nurse. She died September 25, 1913, in Nephi at the age of seventy. Her granddaughter, Marjorie Pay Hinckley, is the wife of President Gordon B. Hinckley of the First Presidency of The Church of Jesus Christ of Latter-day Saints.

SOURCES: Mary Goble Pay. Autobiographical sketch, typescript. LDS Church Archives.

See also "My Story." *In Treasures of Pioneer History,* 4:202–6.

Susan Noble (Grant)

Born: July 25, 1832, Sheldon, Genessee, New York
Parents: Ezekial and Theodocia Bates Noble
1847: George B. Wallace Company
Age at time of journey: 15

In the above photograph, Susan Noble Grant is seated at center.
Susan begins her reminiscence by telling of traveling alongside Captain Jedediah M. Grant's family through central Wyoming. After crossing the North Platte River, they moved southwest to the Sweetwater River, a three-day journey through very unpleasant country. The soil contained much alkali, a salty chemical, which made vegetation sparse and the water nasty and poisonous to drink.

My, how we boys and girls worked day after day to keep our cows and sheep from drinking too large a dose at one time of this brackish water. The weather was so hot, though, and the animals increased in their thirst by the salty country that, in spite of our poundings and pleadings, they would gorge themselves upon the morbific, soap-bubbly stuff and then almost immediately begin being sick. An epidemic of cholera had broken out, spreading first among the animals and then attacking the people, especially the children. As the days passed and the conditions grew no better, the malady increased in severity. I remember one afternoon when our best milk cow stretched out and died. This was the first of our animals to go. All through camp oxen, horses, sheep, pigs, and even the chickens were affected alike. As the human sick list grew, greater loads were added to the weary cattle. Oh, it was just terrible! The vomiting and purging and the knifelike cramps that sapped the vitality in just a few hours, bringing some of the strongest to the wagons and keeping them there for days and finally leaving them pale and weak.

But hope was before us. The Sweetwater River, they declared, was just a day or so ahead. This was a clear, sparkling river running eastward from the Rocky Mountains. As our wagon was close to Captain Jedediah Grant's, I remember how worried he was and how he prayed at our evening meetings that the animals and people would be spared to reach our new home in the mountains. But I guess he didn't pray much harder than some of the women folk, for they had charge of a number of the outfits, hitching and unhitching the oxen and waiting on the sick as well. You see, their husbands and oldest sons, having left the year before with the Mormon Battalion, were now fighting to help bring into the Union the land toward which we were headed. Brigham Young was so sure that all the country westward would belong to the United States that he kept Jedediah Grant from joining Brigham Young's first company by sending him east on important business. He instructed him to buy material for a huge Stars and Stripes flag that should wave over our new homes toward the Pacific. This cloth was later made into a mammoth flag that waved for years over Salt Lake City.

As I was saying, we were close to Captain Grant. His wife, Caroline, was exceptionally kind to me, inviting me often to fix our supper with her. Then in the evening, I helped tend Sister Grant's two little girls, Caroline (whom we called "Caddie"), age two years, and Margaret, age six months. I was regularly charmed with Brother Grant's talks, many of which were from his experiences with the Prophet Joseph. At times, as he spoke, he seemed to be so filled with the inspiration of heaven, that all present thrilled with emotions of testimony. We young people often had the chance to express our own feelings in these little meetings around the prairie campfires.

Oh, children, you do not know how happy we were, even during these severe days of hardest trials! As young as I was, I knew the gospel had been restored. More than once I had heard Joseph Smith declare that our Heavenly Father and his Son Jesus, the resurrected Savior, had come and talked with him. To this day this testimony has never left me. And when I am gone, I want you to tell this to your children and grandchildren.

In spite of our faith and prayers, while we were still in the "salertus country," several children died. Think of holding a little short service, moving forward and leaving the fresh mound in the dim distance. Mothers' hearts were almost broken at such trials.

Sorrow now visited our captain's wagon. Sister Grant had not been very well for several days, and little Margaret got the cholera. And by sundown she was seized with violent spasms. I was so worried, I stayed close by their wagon while I took care of Caddie, the older girl. As night came on, Margaret grew worse. About midnight I was sent to my bed, but later as I looked out, I could still see the parents, accompanied by Sisters Eliza R. Snow and Rebecca W. Riter and Brother and Sister Noble, working with the child by the fire on the sheltered side of their wagon.

The hot weather had brought on a thunderstorm, the first for days. A terrible wind was springing up from the west, driving the loose clay dust before it. In just a few minutes the downpour was upon us. The fires sizzled briefly and were forced out; everyone hurried for shelter. The gale, resembling a hurricane, roared through the country with terrific speed, bringing sheetlike columns of rain in alarming force against the wagon. Several tents were toppled over and almost blown away, while the drenched occupants in their night clothing raced to safer abodes. The storm seemed to be coming from the mountains. After a little it slackened, yet it kept up most of the night. Worried but weary, I finally went off to sleep.

The next morning when I awoke, the sun was shining brightly on my wagon cover. Margaret flashed immediately into my mind. I quickly sat up. No one else had been to bed in our wagon. I was ashamed that I had gone to sleep. Outside I could hear low voices, and I learned that we were to move on to the Sweetwater River before making breakfast. Just then, from the wagon next to ours, I heard little Caddie calling, half lone-somelike, for her mother. I was only half dressed but I was soon ready, and scrambling out, stood for a moment looking about from the wagon tongue. One quick glance and I read part of the sorrow the night had left behind. Over on the side of a rolling clay hill about a stone's throw away, and half surrounded by people, principally women, was a new little mound. Nearer me, the men were busy in the slippery clay, hitching up the cattle for moving. Climbing quickly into Sister Grant's wagon, I threw myself by the side of Caddie, sobbing as only a heartbroken girl can. After a little I heard the folks return-ing. Then, as I waited, I thought of that cold burial, and I knew there had been no mate-rial for a box of any sort—oh, it was terrible!

Brother Grant's animals were now hitched to his wagon. I then heard Brother Riter suggest quietly, "Brother Grant, Sister Riter will ride with Caroline and Caddie this morning. Caroline is not well and must be relieved from all care and further worry." As I softly climbed from the wagon, Brother and Sister Grant saw me. Sister Grant exclaimed, "Oh, Susan!" and throwing her arms around me, she gave expression to her feelings, weeping as if her heart would break.

That morning as we moved forward, the trail proved heavy and slippery. Every gully was chockfull of mud and debris, forced there by the storm of the night before. The air that morning, though, was cool and invigorating. Such a wonderful change nat-urally revived our spirits. By noon we were on the Sweetwater River. The Badlands, like a departing nightmare, lay grim in the distance behind us. A much-needed rest, with plenty of good feed for the animals and a river of clear, fresh water for all, revived the sick and again set us thinking of the mountains.

About noon (September 8), like messengers from another world, three men came riding into camp from the West, members of the Quorum of the Twelve, with Brigham Young at the head. Following them were their well-equipped outfits. They had found us a home by the inland sea, they declared, and were now on their way back to Winter Quarters, Nebraska, to lead out in the general movement in the early spring, wherein thousands of people would make their way westward. You should have seen the meeting of Jedediah Grant and Brigham Young and Heber C. Kimball; why, they just hugged each other like youngsters; Heber and Jedediah were not counselors to Brigham then, but they were later. You see, Brigham was not sustained as President of the Church until he arrived back in Winter Quarters.

The trail from here to South Pass, a hundred miles or more, was all upgrade, but after this splendid rest we moved forward rapidly. Sister Grant was so improved that she walked a little each day. Most of the other sick were rapidly gaining in strength. We had heard so much of South Pass that we thought, of course, a dangerous and difficult climb was before us. One can hardly imagine our surprised feeling when we found the Continental Divide a long, broad, easy upland valley with splendid trails. It was hardly believable until we saw the waters of the Sandy [evidently a small stream] running westward toward Green River.

As our hopes were now flying high, many a teamster shouted, including the women. All felt they had a right to be happy, looking forward and not backward. As our wagons rolled easily along, all joined in singing many a trail song. I'll sing you two or three, but of course I can't make them thrill you as they did us in those days:

> Cheer up, brothers, as we go over the mountains westward ho,
> Where herds of deer and buffalo furnish the fare.
>
> We'll stay on the farm and we'll suffer no loss,
> For the stone that keeps rolling will gather no moss.
>
> Oh, wife, let us go; oh, don't let us wait;
> I long to be there, and I long to be great;
> While you, some fair lady, and who knows but I
> May be some rich governor long 'fore I die.

Our soaring spirits were soon to return, however, and hug the ground in silence, for joys seem to ebb and flow with sorrows ever present. In just a few days, "mountain fever" had confined a great number of people to their wagons. It was with difficulty that the sick could ride at all, for the roads became but trails and were rough and difficult.

Sister Grant, full of faith and hopeful determination, fought off the first signs of the mountain fever, but as she was weakened from the effects of cholera and deep sorrow, back it came with alarming consequences. It was with difficulty now that we could travel at all.

As Sister Grant's condition became rather critical Saturday, she and her bed were gently transferred to a tent that was set up nearby. Sunday brought a higher fever and complete delirium. For the first Sunday on our long journey there was no singing, preaching, or music heard in camp. These were replaced by fasting and prayer for Caroline's recovery. As Brother Grant was a very sympathetic man, this grief, added to the worry and sorrows of the past, was almost more than he could bear. Brother Grant often took Caddie from me, hugging and kissing her while the tears ran down his face.

During the evening of Sunday, as I sat near the fire at the tent door with little Caddie on my lap, I watched carefully the language expressed in the eyes of the attendants. Later on, when the child went to sleep, I was quietly taking her toward my wagon to tuck her away from the cool mountain air when Sister Snow caught up to me, and as she handed me a shawl, she exclaimed a little anxiously, "No, don't take her away." Not until then did it really dawn upon me that there seemed to be no hope. Wrapping the shawl about me and the sleeping child, I sat waiting in silence. About midnight Sister Grant rallied a little and whispered, "Susan—Caddie." I sprang up so quickly when I was called that I woke the little girl, who opened her big eyes and stared about on every side. In a moment we were both by the bed, while Caddie kissed her mama and tried to huddle into the covers. Sister Grant looked at us knowingly; then as she contently closed her eyes again and seemed to be sinking, I heard her whisper to Jedediah, "All is well! All is well! Please take me to the Valley, Jeddy. Get baby Margaret—bring her to me!" Brother Grant answered tenderly as he sobbed with sorrow, "Yes, yes, Caroline. I'll do my best. I'll do my best."

During the night the sisters prepared the body of Sister Grant in the very best manner possible, and the brethren made a box from one of the top beds of the wagon. And with the first dawn of daylight we were hurrying toward the Salt Lake Valley, which was reached three days later on the evening of July 29th. Here the whole group was thrown into intense sorrow, as Sister Grant had been with the Church almost from the beginning. The services were held that evening, and early the next morning the first white woman to be buried in the Salt Lake Valley was quietly laid to rest.

Susan Noble's birth parents were Charles Fairchild and Eunice Noble, but she was adopted and reared by her maternal grandparents, Ezekial and Theodocia Noble. Susan later became the wife of Captain Jedediah Grant, marrying him February 11, 1849. They became the parents of two children, a boy and a girl. They adopted a boy, Lewis McKeachie, whose parents had died crossing the Great Plains, and the Grants also raised a girl, Bertha Zahler, from Switzerland. Bertha's parents sent her to Utah in care of LDS missionaries, and she was taken into the Grant household. Susan lovingly reared "Caddie," daughter of Jedediah and his deceased wife, Caroline. After Jedediah's death in 1856, Susan married his brother, George D. Grant, by whom she had a son. Susan became president of the Davis Stake Relief Society and later served as a member of the Relief Society General Board from 1892 to 1914. She died March 7, 1914, in Bountiful, Davis County, Utah.

SOURCE: Carter E. Grant. "Robbed by Wolves, a True Story." *Relief Society Magazine* 15 (July 1928): 355–64.

Part Six

LIFE ON THE PLAINS

"I will take you one of a city, and two of a family, and I will bring you to Zion."

❧ JEREMIAH 3:14

Historians have called the Mormon migration the best-organized movement of people in American history. The Mormons were transplanting an entire people, a culture, not just isolated, unrelated individuals. They moved to the Salt Lake Valley as villages on wheels.

Church leaders organized each company into groups of tens, fifties, and hundreds, and provided leaders for each group. Some men were appointed to scout out the trail ahead and others to ride along the front, sides, and rear—guarding and enclosing the moving camp in an orderly formation. For safety's sake neither people nor animals could be allowed to stray from the group.

Brigham Young laid out what the daily routine of each pioneer camp should be:

> At 5 o'clock in the morning the bugle is to be sounded as a signal for every man to arise and attend prayers before he leaves his wagon. Then the people will engage in cooking, eating, feeding teams, etc., until seven o'clock, at which time the train is to move at the sound of the bugle. Each teamster is to keep beside his team with loaded gun in hand or within easy reach, while the extra men, observing the same rule regarding their weapons, are to walk by the side of the particular wagons to which they belong; and no man may leave his post without the permission of his officers. In case of an attack or any hostile demonstration by Indians, the wagons will travel in double file—the order of encampment to be in a circle, with the mouth of each wagon to the outside and the horses and cattle tied inside the circle. At half past eight each evening the bugles are to be sounded again, upon which signal all will hold prayers in their wagons, and be retired to rest by nine o'clock. (William Clayton's journal, entry for April 18, 1847, quoted in B. H. Roberts, A Comprehensive History of The Church of Jesus Christ of Latter-day Saints, 6 vols. [Provo: Brigham Young University Press, 1965], 3:165–66.)

There were other camp rules as well. Travelers were not to abuse their cattle but to treat them properly. They were not to yell or cry out or make any noise, nor were they to be up at night. They were to put out fires and tie up their hogs and dogs.

Such camp organization was chiefly the result of a revelation to Brigham Young, published as Section 136 of the Doctrine and Covenants. It begins, "The Word and Will of the Lord concerning the Camp of Israel in their journeyings to the West," and out-lines with inspired conviction the ideals of faith, obedience, sacrifice, mutual support, and joyfulness that made both the crossing of the plains and the settling of the Great Basin possible.

❧

SARAH SOPHIA MOULDING (GLEDHILL)

Born: March 7, 1858, Philadelphia, Pennsylvania
Parents: William Henry and Eliza Wickens Moulding
1861: William Andrews "Independent" Company
Age at time of journey: 3

Before we began our journey to the Salt Lake Valley, the men, including my father, had to go to the corrals and practice driving the ox-teams, as it was an entirely new occupation for them. The idle men of the town hung around to watch and make fun of them, but the Mormons had lots of pep and soon learned. They also knew they would have to walk most of the thousand miles to Utah, but they bravely undertook the task.

We came in what was called an independent company, but it was well organized, having a leader for every four or five wagons. We had a hard trip, but I never heard my parents complain of it when telling me about it later.

I was just past three years of age when we made the trip, and Ida, my sister, was about four and a half. Mother was not very well when we started on the trip, having just recovered from the smallpox and having the new baby. She was very pale, but the fresh air seemed to help her a lot, and she too was able to walk most all the way.

The covered wagon was heavily loaded, and the older ones had to walk to make the load lighter. In our wagon were two large wooden boxes, or chests, filled to overflowing with clothing, dishes, Father's tools for his business, and numerous other articles. In the back of the wagon was fastened the sheet-iron stove, cooking utensils, and our food. On top of the chests was placed bedding of all kinds, and on top of all this we three children had our living quarters during most of the trip. As little as I was, I can remember the noise of the wagon and the jingle-jangle of the pots and kettles fastened underneath and at the sides of the wagon. I remember the dust and dirt from the wagons in front of us.

We were so thirsty, and the only time we could stop and get a drink from the canteen that father carried over his shoulder was when the other wagons stopped. Everyone had been warned to keep up with the wagons and not stray behind on account of the Indians. When we did stop to get a drink, I would always have to wait until my sister had her drink because in England, where my parents were from, the older child was always favored and came first in everything. I can remember how I would dance up and down waiting for her to finish getting her drink, and how thirsty I was. The water was warm and never very good. And at times the water was terrible because they would have to dig a hole to get it, and then it would be muddy.

The baby cried a good deal of the time from being bounced around in the wagon so much, and we two girls often cried in sympathy with him. The meals were about the same and very tiresome; the bread was poor, and we didn't have butter. It was hard to bake bread, crossing the plains. They would set up the stoves and probably just get a fire started when the wind would come up, and away would go the stove pipe.

At night they had their times of enjoyments, holding meetings and singing songs of Zion. They even danced once in a while. We girls would get out and play with a little girl in the next wagon, who had a set of dishes made of lead. The red ants were so bad, and Mother often had to strip off our clothes to get rid of them, and how they did bite!

As we got closer to Utah, we children could only look out of the front end of the wagons, and all we could see was the ever-present thistle and skunkweed that grew just beside the road. I remember getting such a dislike for them, and to this day I cannot stand the sight of the color. Mother used to hate the mountains when we first came to Utah, and I guess it was because they seemed to shut her away from her folks in England. She finally became accustomed to them, and later on she loved them just as we children did.

After reaching the Salt Lake Valley, I remember seeing one of the last companies of handcart pioneers when they arrived after crossing the plains. They walked onto the Eighth Ward square, and groups of children were out to see them, peeking through cracks in the high board fence.

One family in particular attracted my attention: there was the father, mother and two children about twelve and thirteen years of age. The father was cooking over the open fire, and the mother was sitting down on the ground near the handcart. The children were passing things from the mother to the father for him to cook. The man was the thinnest, most ragged I have ever seen. His sleeves were in tatters to the elbow, and his pants were rags to the knees. The handcart pioneers all looked like Indians, they were so brown from exposure.

⌒⌒

Sarah S. Moulding safely reached the Salt Lake Valley in late September 1861. She married Adam Gledhill in 1887. They settled in Ogden, Utah, and became the parents of two children. Sarah owned property at 28th Street and Pingree Avenue in Ogden. She had four homes built on the property, which she rented for extra income. She gave her son one of the homes as a wedding gift. She was an excellent hat maker and worked at the post office in Ogden. Sarah died December 30, 1952, at the age of ninety-four, in Roy, Utah.

SOURCE: Sarah S. Moulding Gledhill. Autobiography, typescript. Special Collections, Merrill Library, Utah State University Library, Logan, Utah.

Mary Jane Mount (Tanner)

Born: February 27, 1837, Toledo, Lucas, Ohio
Parents: Joseph and Elizabeth Bessac Mount
1847: Abraham O. Smoot Company
Age at time of journey: 10

I think I shall never forget that long lonely day after leaving Nauvoo, Illinois, waiting on that vast, undulating prairie that stretched as far as the eye could reach, covered with grass and flowers. It must have been a lovely scene that bright spring morning, but I hardly think it was properly appreciated by the little band who were so bravely leaving home, friends, country, and kindred to take their toilsome march across the Rocky Mountains.

The oxen were detached from the wagons and feeding lazily among the green grass, knowing nothing of the future that lay before them, or that before many months their bones would, many of them, whiten on the desert sands. My childish heart knew as little as they of the hardship that lay before us. My pale, delicate mother watched the teams while my father busied himself assisting or counseling those who were starting out. No doubt her heart failed her on that long weary day as she sat in the bright spring sunshine, watching the shadows and thinking of all she was leaving behind and wondering what the future held in store for her.

I used to see other children running along barefooted and thought it would be nice to take my shoes off too. But my feet were not accustomed to such rough usage, and I was generally glad to put them on again. One day while trying the experiment, I wandered a little way from the road and, getting among a bed of prickly pears, was obliged to sit down and take care of my feet while some of the children went to the wagon for my shoes. As the wagons kept traveling on, this threw me some distance behind our team, and I was considerably fatigued by the time I caught up. I think this must have cured me of the desire to go barefooted.

There were a great many ant hills along the road raised to a considerable height, where we often found beads which were, no doubt, lost by the Indians and collected by those indefatigable little workers along with the gravel of which their mounds were composed. If we were hardy enough to risk a bite now and then, we found much amusement in searching for the beads to string into necklaces.

Another favorite pastime consisted of walking far enough ahead of the train to get a little time to play, when we would drive the huge crickets—large, unwieldy insects, if they could be called such—that abounded in some sections of the country, and build corrals of sand or rocks to put them in, calling them our cattle.

Halfway through the Mounts' journey, the young boy hired to drive their wagon returned to Winter Quarters, leaving Mary's mother, Elizabeth, to drive the team.

Mother drove the team the rest of the way, yoking and unyoking in addition to her other duties. One of her oxen would never learn to hold back, and when going downhill she had to hold his horn with one hand and pound his nose with the other to keep him from running into the wagon ahead of him, a feat which would astonish some of our belles of the present day, and yet she was reared as tenderly and as little accustomed to hardship as any of them. Many times the bushes caught her dress, and she had no choice but to rush on, leaving it in pieces behind her. I wonder if those coming after her knew what those tattered rags meant.

We arrived in Salt Lake Valley in late September, 1847. The valley presented a barren aspect; it was covered mostly with sagebrush and sunflowers, with a few small streams of water running through it and some squalid Indian wigwams scattered about.

❧

Mary Jane Mount married Myron Tanner in 1856, and they lived in Peteetneet, afterwards known as Payson, Utah. They became parents of nine children. Mary Jane loved writing and wrote articles for the Woman's Exponent. *She fulfilled a lifelong dream when she published a collection of her poetry,* Fugitive Poems, *in 1880. She served as a Relief Society president in Provo for twenty-two years. She died January 8, 1890, at the age of fifty-three. She was the grandmother of prominent Utah philanthropist Obert C. Tanner.*

SOURCES: Mary Jane Mount Tanner. Autobiography; Reminiscences and Diary. LDS Church Archives.

See also *A Fragment: The Autobiography of Mary Jane Mount Tanner,* edited by Mary Jane Mount Tanner with George S. Tanner. Utah, the Mormons, and the West [Series], no. 9. Salt Lake City: University of Utah Library, 1980.

WILLIAM HENRY FRESHWATER

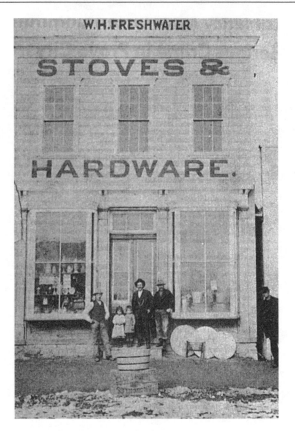

Born: May 23, 1852, Hertford, England
Parents: William and Martha Gootch Freshwater
1863: William B. Preston Company
Age at time of journey: 11

In the above photograph, William Henry Freshwater is the adult standing in front of the door of his store.

May 8, 1862. We left Hertford, England, my native city and country, with several other Latter-day Saints, all enroute for Utah, U.S.A.

May 10th. We left Watford, England, at 8 a.m. by railroad. We passed through several tunnels; in one of them Mother fainted. We took berth on a sailing ship named *William Tapscott,* which was bound for New York, America.

May 13th. The ship raised anchor and left the dock with seven hundred and eighty-five Mormons on board and went into the River Mersey. Two accidents occurred today. One, a boy fell from the main deck to the lower and broke his leg very bad; the other, a woman, in coming down the hatchway, slipped and spilled some boiling water on the face of a child. The vessel was towed out of the river by steam tug into the Irish Sea. The weather is beautiful and warm.

May 15th. A few of the passengers are a little seasick. There were two boys found in the hold, and Captain Preston is going to make them work their passage across the sea.

June 8th. In the morning, wind very fair but during the day it increased until the sailors had to tie ropes about the ship to hold themselves on. They spiked all the hatchways down and would not let any of the passengers go on deck at all. The captain told us it was the worst storm he had ever witnessed although he had made many trips across the ocean.

June 24th. We arrived in the mouth of the Hudson River, at four o'clock and dropped anchor at five. This is a very beautiful port. Far excels Liverpool, England.

June 25th. We were all up at the first peep of day and anxiously awaiting the arrival of the examining doctor, who came at 8 a.m. and pronounced us all well except two who remained on board the ship, the last we heard of them. The steam tug took us to Castle Garden, the New York immigrant landing where one can stay for ten days only.

William and his parents and sister lived and worked in New York City eleven months until they had earned enough money to go on to Utah.

June 26, 1863. In company with my father, mother, and sister, Valora, I left Williamsburg, New York with a company of Mormon immigrants for Great Salt Lake City, Utah. Just before we arrived in St. Joseph, Missouri, the rebels, or bushwhackers, fired two cannonballs through our train. One shot went through the passenger car, exactly eight inches above the people's heads, and the other through a baggage car, destroying a great amount of baggage. We stayed in St. Joseph three or four days, afraid to go on because of the rebel soldiers being all through the country.

While we were there, some fifteen rebel soldiers were taken prisoner, right from among our company, by the northern soldiers. Two companies of Union soldiers surrounded the depot and made the rebels surrender, or they would have killed them. I can truly say I saw a little of the War between the North and the South.

July 9, 1863. We started across the plains with a train of fifty wagons drawn by three to five yoke of cattle; some of them were trail wagons. The Platte River was very high. We had considerable trouble in crossing several streams. We had several heavy storms; one I remember was near Chimney Rock, in Nebraska, a lot of lightning and thunder. Our cattle stampeded and started running away. The teamsters unyoked them as best they could, some of them two and three yoked together. Three of the oxen were dragged to death. That night, herders went after them on horses.

Devil's Gate, in Wyoming, was quite a scenic place. The wagon train went around and up a canyon, but most of the passengers went over the mountain. When we got over and into the valley on the west, the sagebrush was as large as fence poles and eight to ten feet high.

We arrived in Great Salt Lake City Thursday, September 15th, 1863, just as the peaches were ripe. We stayed in Salt Lake three days and visited all the main places. The temple was then about four feet high.

❧

William Henry Freshwater married Sarah Ann Davies, and they became the parents of eight children. He owned and operated a successful hardware store on Center Street in Provo. He was short and stocky, always kept a diary, and enjoyed fishing and playing cards with his children and grandchildren. He was known for his honesty, and his generosity helped many families through the Great Depression. William Freshwater died January 27, 1937, in Provo, Utah, at the age of eighty-four.

SOURCE: William Henry Freshwater, "From His Diary," in *Our Pioneer Heritage*, comp. Kate B. Carter, 20 vols. (Salt Lake City: Daughters of Utah Pioneers, 1964), 7:248–52.

LUCINA MECHAM (BOREN)

Born: March 11, 1841, Lee County, Iowa
Parents: Moses Worthen and Elvira Derby Mecham
1853: John Brown Company
Age at time of journey: 12

The above photograph shows Lucina Mecham Boren with her grandchildren.

Just a short time before the Prophet Joseph Smith was killed, he came to our place in Nauvoo, Illinois. He took me on his knee; I was too young to remember what he said, but I can remember him holding me on his knee. When we were out playing and he happened to pass, everyone stopped playing to watch him until he was out of sight.

I shall never forget when Mother took me and my baby sister, Elvira, to see the Prophet and Patriarch Hyrum Smith after they were killed by the mob. Mother did not want to take me, as I had no shoes, but I wanted to go. She said, "I will take you so you can always remember you saw the Prophet and his brother." The night they were killed, the dogs were howling all night. The people of Nauvoo beat their drums to let the mob know we were on the lookout for them, and now I am eighty-three years old, but I cannot help crying whenever I hear a dog howl or a drum beat.

While we were in Nauvoo, I was burned very bad, then caught cold and was very sick. Father was not home. Mother sent for the elders, and a Brother Goddard came and administered to me. He told Mother to wilt a cabbage leaf and put it on the burn, and I would be all right. I never suffered any more pain, and I have had faith in the elders ever since.

The day we left Nauvoo, we had not had flour for weeks. Father purchased a little white flour and Mother made some light bread. We children were so anxious to eat we would keep asking how long it would be until we could eat. Our dear patient mother did not get angry with us as most mothers do, but when we did get to eat, what a feast it was: white bread and milk from old Muley! Never have I had such a dinner.

One day a woman came to Uncle Ephraim with a pig's ham to sell. Aunt Polly, his wife, said she did not have anything to pay for it. Afterwards Aunt Polly said she did not like the looks of it. In a few days a friend told Aunt Polly that the pig had died of "collory" and the woman had said it would be good to kill the Mormons with.

We moved to Kanesville, now Council Bluffs, Iowa, where my father took up some land one and one-half miles from Kanesville. We had just got settled when a flood came and took about everything we had. We then built a house on a hill, where we had to carry water three-fourths of a mile. I well remember how frightened we were going through the woods, as some of the men had killed a wild cat. We picked wild grapes, strawberries, raspberries, gooseberries, blackberries, elderberries, also walnuts, hazelnuts, hickory nuts, and butternuts. Thus I earned my first pair of shoes. Up to this time my mother had made moccasins out of buckskins.

We moved to Kanesville, Iowa, in 1847. My mother cut her hand very badly, and her only sister, Aunt Polly Mecham, came to see her. She took Mother to her place for three weeks. While she was there, my brother made her a cupboard, and we girls bought and filled it with dishes, and oh! how happy she was when she returned.

In the spring of 1853 we started for Utah. We went a long way on a raft. I was always afraid of water. We crossed the Missouri River on a ferry boat, which frightened me very much, as the water was very high.

We left the Missouri River July 18th. My father started with two wagons, one yoke of oxen, two yoke of unbroken steers, and four cows. The man that sold Father the oxen had stolen them, and the man that he had stolen them from came and took them from us, so we only had one wagon and the cows.

The Indians were on the warpath, so we all had to travel together for safety. We were stopped once by the Indians. I thought there were one thousand of them! They could easily have killed us all, but we gave them provisions by robbing ourselves and then suffering from want of food.

We children had to walk most of the way. We stopped one day each week for wash-day, and we were always allowed time to keep ourselves clean. When we camped at night, the first wagon would stop. The next wagon would stop at his side, and so on, till they were all in a circle making a corral of the wagons and we would stay inside for safety. After supper and the animals were taken care of, we would sit around the fire, sing songs, tell stories, and those that were not too tired would dance. One brother had a violin, and he was very good at it for dancing.

My sister Sarah and I stopped to rest one day, and the wagons passed us. Sarah said she was not going any farther. I begged her to come with me, but she said she would rather be eaten by wolves than go on. She tried to get me to go and catch the wagons, but I told her I would not leave her. Then she said, "I will not see the wolves get you, so come on, let us go to camp."

When we were three days from Salt Lake, my cousin Daniel Mecham met us with a load of food, flour, meat, and vegetables. And what a godsend it was, for we were out of food. The next day Brother Allen I. Stout, a friend of ours, came with another load of food. We all rode in the extra wagons to Salt Lake. We arrived October 16, 1853.

❧

Lucina Mecham married William Jasper Boren July 3, 1859, in Provo, Utah. They became the parents of thirteen children, living in Wallsburg, Utah County, Utah. Lucina became a midwife and delivered over five hundred babies. At the age of fifty, she took music lessons and became the ward organist. She also ran a small mercantile store and worked in the Manti Temple. She died June 21, 1925, at the age of eighty-four.

SOURCE: "Journal of Lucina Mecham Boren." In *Treasures of Pioneer History*, 6:301–48.

CATHERINE ADAMS (PILLING)

Born: April 9, 1838, Payson Township, Adams, Illinois
Parents: Elias and Malinda Railey Adams
1850: Aaron Johnson "Independent" Company
Age at time of journey: 12

It was in the spring of 1850 that we started for Utah. Our party was the smallest that ever crossed the plains. There were seventeen or eighteen wagons.

The buffalo were thick in those days. We used to kill one now and again, but we had to wait till one wandered away from the herd. Instead of frightening them away, the sound of the gun seemed to infuriate them so that they stampeded and charged right for camp, where they'd go pell-mell over everything in their way, wagons, animals, everything. The buffalo doesn't run, you know, he lopes. And when a large herd is moving in the distance, it looks like a small, dark mountain swaying. They stay close together and seldom stray. They didn't try to keep out of our way.

We were always afraid of Indians. But our party was fortunate in not running into many of them nor having them run into us. Once we had quite a fright: eight or ten warriors came into camp. They were painted in all their savage, hideous war paint, but they were sober, which was a blessing. It was the liquor that made the Indians so dangerous in those days. Father got talking with them and gave them some food. It wasn't food they were after; it was ammunition. But we only had enough for our own use, and Father didn't give them any.

My father was fairly well-to-do, and we traveled in covered wagons. We didn't have to use the pushcart [handcart] in our outfit, as so many had to do. The pushcart, you know, is almost like a big wheelbarrow, but it holds a mighty heavy load. The men would get between the handles and pull it while the women and children pushed. The widows who crossed had to pull their own. It was terribly tiring and tedious in the hot and rainy weather, especially through the part of the country where one could travel for days without seeing even a bunch of willows.

We had many good times, though. In the evenings after the horses were tethered the men would light a big bonfire, clear off a level piece of ground, dampen it down to pack it a bit, and have a dance. There were some fine musicians along who played the fiddle, mouth organ, and accordion, and we used to enjoy sitting around the fire listening to them or having a sing-song.

Instead of cooking on a stove, father used to dig a trench about a foot wide in the sod to set the kettle on. We'd fill the trench with buffalo chips and cook our meals over it.

The way we made our butter was we'd milk the cows in the morning and strain the milk into large churns, which were put in the back of the wagons. At night, through the constant motion of the wagon all day, there would be pieces of rich yellow butter clinging to the sides of the churn; some of them would be the size of goose eggs.

We reached Utah in September. There was mighty little there at that time; in fact, it looked like a pretty discouraging country to settle in and try to raise a garden or crop of any kind.

We were still concerned about Indians. There was one old Indian in the neighborhood who used to chase women. We were all terrified of him. This one day when my mother and my brother George went to the grist mill, the Indian tried to climb into our wagon. George couldn't make the team go fast because he had a heavy load, and while he drove, Mother took a club and beat the old Indian's hands with it every time he tried to climb over the end of the wagon.

❧

Catherine Adams married Richard Pilling March 10, 1856, in Salt Lake City. The couple became the parents of eleven children. They lived in Layton, Utah, until 1889, when they moved to Cardston, Alberta, Canada, where they were involved in ranching. Richard was bishop of the Aetna Ward. Catherine served as a Relief Society president and as a temple worker at the LDS Temple in Cardston. She was an excellent and trusted midwife, assisting in the birth of over five hundred babies in Alberta. She died October 1, 1935, in Cardston.

SOURCES: G. A. Skov. "From Handcart to Airplane." *Deseret News,* April 4, 1931.

See also *Ancestors and Descendants of Elias Adams: The Pioneer, 600–1930,* compiled and edited by Frank D. Adams. Kaysville, Utah: F. D. Adams, 1929.

MARGARET MCNEIL (BALLARD)

Born: April 14, 1846, Tranent, East Lothian, Scotland
Parents: Thomas and Janet Reid McNeil
1859: John McNeil "Independent" Company
Age at the time of journey: 13

In the above photograph, Margaret Ballard is holding her twins.

The first ten years of my life were spent in Tranent, Scotland. Because of being a "Mormon," I was not permitted to attend the schools, and so I was entirely deprived of schooling while in the old country. My father was a coal miner and had to be to work every morning at four A.M. Therefore, when I was baptized, I had to go very early in the morning. It was a beautiful May morning when I walked to the seashore. We carried a lantern to light our way. As I came up out of the water, day was just beginning to dawn, and the light to creep up over the eastern hills. It was a beautiful sight. That night the Saints met at our house, and I was confirmed a member of the Church.

On April 27, 1856, we left Liverpool, England, for America. There was a large company leaving. My mother was not well and was taken on board ship before the time of sailing, while the sailors were still disinfecting and renovating the ship. Here my brother Charles was born, with only one woman on board to attend to my mother.

When the captain and doctor came on board the ship and found that a baby had been born, they were delighted and thought it would bring good luck to the company. They asked the privilege of naming him. Brother James G. Willie, president of the company, thought it best to let the captain name him as there were three hundred passengers and nearly all of them were Mormons, so he was named Charles Collins Thornton McNeil, after the ship *Thornton* and Captain Charles Collins.

We were six weeks on the voyage. We landed at Castle Garden, New York. We were planning to go to Utah with the handcart company, but Franklin D. Richards counseled my father not to go in that company, for which we were afterwards thankful because of the great suffering and privations, and cold weather which these people were subject to. There were many of the company who were frozen that year on the plains.

They made their first stop in St. Louis, Missouri, and later, with other Saints, assisted in settling a place called Genoa, which was one hundred miles west of present-day Omaha, Nebraska. Along the way, the McNeils' team, which consisted of unbroken five-year-old oxen, ran away, and they were delayed.

The company had gone ahead, and my mother was anxious to have me go with them; so she strapped my little brother, James, on my back with a shawl. He was only four years old and was still quite sick with the measles. Mother had all she could do to care for the other children, so I hurried on and caught up with the company.

I traveled with them all day, and that night a kind lady helped me take my brother off my back. I sat up and held him in my lap with a shawl wrapped around him, alone all night. We traveled this way for about a week, my brother and I not seeing our mother during this time. Each morning one of the men would write a note and put it in the slit of a willow stuck in the ground to tell how we were getting along. The people in the camp were very good to us and gave us a little fried bacon and some bread for breakfast.

Soon our family was reunited and began our trek across the plains in 1859. While crossing the plains, my mother's health was very poor, so I tried to assist her as much as I could. Every morning I would rise early and get breakfast for the family and milk my cow so that I could hurry and drive her on ahead of the company. Then I would let her eat in all the grassy places until the company had passed on ahead, when I would hurry and catch up with them. The cow furnished us with milk, our chief source of food, and it was very important to see that she was fed as well as circumstances would permit. Had it not been for the milk, we would have starved.

Being alone much of the time, I had to get across the rivers the best I could. Our cow was a Jersey and had a long tail. When it was necessary to cross a river, I would wind the end of the cow's tail around my hand and swim across with her. At the end of each day's journey I would milk her and help prepare our supper and then would be glad to go to sleep wherever my bed happened to be. Our food gave out, and we had nothing but milk and wild rose berries to eat. However, we had a good team and could travel fast.

One night our cow ran away from camp, and I was sent to bring her back. I was not watching where I was going and was barefooted. All of a sudden I began to feel I was walking on something soft. I looked down to see what it could be, and to my horror found that I was standing in a bed of snakes, large ones and small ones. At the sight of them I became so weak I could scarcely move; all I could think of was to pray, and in some way I jumped out of them. The Lord blessed and cared for me.

We arrived in Ogden, Utah, on the fourth day of October, after a journey of hardships and hunger, with thankfulness to our Heavenly Father for his protecting care. I walked every step of the way across the plains and drove a cow, and a large part of the way I carried my brother, James, on my back.

We camped on the outskirts of town while Father went on into Ogden to find work. Across the field from where we were was a little house, and out in the yard was a big pile of squash. We were all nearly starved to death. My mother sent me over to this place to beg a squash, for we did not have a cent of money, and some of the children were very weak for the want of food. I knocked at the door, and an old lady came and said, "Come in, come in, I knew you were coming and have been told to give you food." She gave me a large loaf of fresh bread and said to tell my mother that she would come over soon. It was not long until she came and brought us a nice cooked dinner, something we had not had for a long time. The woman was surely inspired of the Lord to help us, and we were indeed grateful for her kindness.

❦

Margaret McNeil settled in Cache Valley, Utah, where she married Henry Ballard. She became the mother of eleven children and was a Relief Society president for thirty years. Her husband was bishop for thirty-nine years. One of their sons, Melvin J. Ballard, was called to the Quorum of the Twelve Apostles in 1919, one year after Margaret died. Her great-grandson is Elder M. Russell Ballard, a member of the Quorum of the Twelve Apostles.

Sources: Margaret McNeil Ballard. Autobiography. In *Our Pioneer Heritage*, 3:199–206.

Also, interview in *Utah Pioneer Biographies*, 4:49–50. A fifty-nine-page photocopy of the transcript is in the Harold B. Lee Library, Brigham Young University, Provo, Utah.

LUCY MARIE CANFIELD (MARGETTS)

Born: November 7, 1846, Ossian, Livingston, New York
Parents: Isaac Augustus and Pauline Melissa Smith Canfield
1862: Isaac A. Canfield Company
Age at time of journey: 15

My father, cousin Rose Canfield, and myself left Livingston County, New York, in the spring of 1862 for Salt Lake City. We traveled by rail to Iowa, where we stayed a couple of weeks and got a team of oxen and a wagon. We traveled 150 miles across Iowa by team and stopped in Florence, Nebraska, six miles upriver from Council Bluffs, Iowa. Ours was an independent company, and Father was the captain. We had eighteen wagons in all.

July 2nd. We went down to the boat before breakfast. Al West came and brought us some perfumery.

July 4th. Brigham Kimball brought us a mule to ride. Sewed some on the wagon cover.

July 7th. We had a very hard thunderstorm. Joseph Young was badly hurt.

July 8th. It is a pleasant day. Alvin West and I gathered some wormwood to use for Mr. Young. He is quite bad. Our wagon cover has been repaired.

July 11th. Al went to Omaha and bought Rose and me each a fan.

July 21st. It is a very pleasant day. My poor cousin Rose is so very homesick. Hattie and I try to cheer her.

July 22nd. Brigham Kimball sent Rose a circle comb to cheer her.

July 23rd. Worked on another wagon cover all day.

July 25th. Rose got all ready to go back home, but her heart failed her.

July 27th. Rained last night. Dansie Stickney and I stayed in their tent.

July 30th. Some boys from Ogden, Utah, camped near us. Al was up twice today. His company is about two miles away.

August 2nd. Traveled about eight miles. Broke an axle tree and had to stop.

August 10th. It has not seemed much like Sunday today. We traveled about 15 1/2 miles with no stopping to rest. Camped at Lone Tree, pleasant place.

August 12th. Had a ride with Mrs. Neil about five miles. Crossed Wood River, and had an awful night with the mosquitoes. Got up about midnight and slept on the ground. Do not like Wood River camping very much.

August 23rd. Saw some Indians on horse back. Gave them flour and meat.

Sept. 1st. Made seventeen miles and camped opposite Chimney Rock, Nebraska. 'Tis a wild and romantic country round this rock. There is a stage station near it.

Sept. 4th. Traveled about nine miles. Roasted a duck for our supper.

Sept. 9th. Discovered a dead Indian in a tree this morning. Saw two squaws.

Sept. 19th. Some of the cattle missing. Did not find them until afternoon. Made another buffalo pie.

Sept. 25th. Traveled ten miles before breakfast. Rose and I slept until we got almost to a camping place. Mr. Merrick shot and the men dressed an antelope. We cooked some over our sagebrush fire.

Sept. 28th. Traveled ten miles. Camped near a military station. The soldiers invited some of us to take dinner with them.

Oct. 8th. Went over to the military station. Saw there a tame bear. Joseph West sent us some peaches by Mr. Dickson's brother-in-law.

Oct. 10th. Camped about noon. One of Mr. Elton's mules died. It seemed so bad, for he thought so much of it. Had some soup for our supper, and it was first rate.

Oct. 11th. Took dinner at Cache Cave. Quite a cave. Mrs. Blackman's wagon tongue broke and we camped about 5 P.M., opposite some high bluffs. Went on top, and the boys rolled stones down them. Camped in Echo Canyon, Utah.

Oct. 13th. A beautiful morning. Were ready to start out and found some cattle gone. Our company separated, and we went down the Weber Canyon. We crossed the Weber River five times. Bad roads and bad going. Camped in a valley surrounded by mountains.

Oct. 14th. A very pleasant day. Got started at half past eight o'clock. Most romantic road we have yet had. Would not have missed coming this way for anything. I never saw such rocks, bigger and prettier in shapes than all we saw in Echo Canyon. Camped at Mr. Merrill's. They gave us some butter.

Oct. 15th. Started this morning in quite good season. Forded the Weber three times. Stopped at Mrs. Kempton's and took dinner. Had some peaches to eat and a first-rate dinner. Liked Mrs. Kempton well. We crossed the Weber, and the oxen swam across and we camped on the other side.

Oct. 16th. Started before breakfast. Got to Aunt Hattie's about ten o'clock. Aunt Hattie looks just as natural as can be. Had to empty all the trunks. They were all wet. We dried all and worked fast to get things in shape to pack again.

Oct. 18th. Did not go to the meeting in the forenoon. I thought I could not stand it to go two whole days. Went in the afternoon. Had a good meeting. Heard Brigham Young speak.

Oct. 23rd. It won't be long now if all goes well before we will all be in Salt Lake City.

∽

Twice widowed, Lucy Canfield married John Willard Young, Ara Williams Sabin, and Phillip Henry Margetts. She lived in Ogden and Salt Lake City and later established a boarding house called "The Cottage Hotel" in Preston, Idaho. She was the mother of eight children. Those who knew her described her as lively, strong willed, and a hard worker. She died May 16, 1915, in Preston, Idaho. Lucy Canfield was the great-grandmother of Elder Jack H. Goaslind of the First Quorum of the Seventy of The Church of Jesus Christ of Latter-day Saints. Lucy's cousin Rose became a prominent teacher in Ogden and taught Jeannette Evans (McKay), the mother of President David O. McKay.

Sources: Lucy Marie Canfield Margetts. Diary, holograph. LDS Church Archives.

See also Newell Hart. *Hometown Sketchbook: Preston's Mainstreet in Transition.* Preston, Idaho: Cache Valley Newsletter Publ. Co., 1981.

Part Seven
FUN AND ROMANCE

"*The ransomed of the Lord shall return, and come to Zion with songs and everlasting joy upon their heads: they shall obtain joy and gladness.*"

∽ ISAIAH 35:10

The journey to the Salt Lake Valley was not just endless work. Like children everywhere, young Latter-day Saints were creative in having fun and finding amusements as they walked or rode the trail to Zion. For children, as well as their parents, the prairie and mountains presented a new land of infinite variety to explore. Just as an infant grabs at anything within reach, holds it, tastes it, and learns to discriminate among objects, youngsters on the plains were also anxious to experience fully their new surroundings.

Riding inside the wagons, small boys and girls played with everything around them and, as soon as they could, jumped out to explore the scenes they had been watching for hours. There were colored pebbles and discarded antlers to collect, wild flowers to pick, and prairie dogs to chase. Slightly older children were everywhere—gathering snake skins, beetles, wild berries, and animal dung. Much to their mother's displeasure, they caught (and usually executed) spiders, centipedes, and snakes.

Children also found ways of making their work into play. Teenage girls had contests gathering service berries for pies, and the boys made games out of chopping wood or gathering buffalo chips for the evening fires. They also participated in more organized games such as "Run, Sheepie, Run," "Anti-I-Over," and "Hide 'n' Seek."

In the evening, after finishing the chores of the day, both young and old joined around the campfire for singing, dancing, and listening to someone in the company play the fiddle, harmonica, or trumpet. Under the light of the moon, the young women took their turns bathing in a nearby stream, splashing and having fun, under the watchful eye of a maiden aunt from their camp.

And of course there were romances in these traveling communities. Numerous marriages were performed on the plains, and other couples decided to tie the knot after arriving in the Salt Lake Valley. One thing was certain: courtship on the Great Plains gave both parties a chance to see each other under a variety of unusual and trying circumstances, which meant that there was little chance of being surprised at a spouse's temperament or personality after the marriage ceremony.

ALMA ELIZABETH MINEER (FELT)

Born: May 1, 1855, Landskrona, Malmohus, Sweden
Parents: Andrew and Inger Jensen Mineer
1861: John R. Murdock Company
Age at time of journey: 6

In the above photograph, Alma Mineer Felt is seated at center.

In 1861, Father and Mother sold our lovely home in Sweden and came to Utah. At Liverpool, England, we embarked on *The Monarch of the Sea,* a very old and rickety ship and entirely unseaworthy. The sea was so rough and stormy that the waves washed over the top of the deck. When the people were frightened, the captain said, "We'll land in New York all right. We've got Mormons on board, and we always get through when we have Mormons." On its return voyage, *The Monarch of the Sea,* loaded with cargo, sank, but the captain and the crew were saved.

There were a lot of sailors on the boat, and they were so good to me. A Negro cook who had his kitchen on the upper deck was very kindhearted and generous. He used to give me prunes, dried apples, raisins, and sometimes cookies, and often a little bowl of soup. I was on deck frequently and knew all the sailors and the cook. Sometimes he used to sneak some soup down to the emigrants in the steerage because he felt so sorry for them. The captain caught him at this, and he was put in jail. The jail was on the upper deck, and I can remember that I used to see his black fingers over the bars through the high opening of the door. One day he died. They told me that the captain had starved him to death. The body of my friend, the Negro cook, was brought into the kitchen, where it was sewed up in a sheet. Then they put him on a long board, carried him to the side of the boat, and slid him into the ocean. I was the chief mourner because he had been so good to me.

One day my sister was on deck, and one of the sailors who was up on the mast dropped one of the iron spikes on my sister's head, and the blood was streaming onto the deck. The poor boy did not mean to do it, but some of the officers started to beat him. My mother came up on deck, elbowed her way through the crowd to the boy, and said, "You leave him alone; he never meant to hurt my child!" Although she could not speak the English language, she made herself understood in Swedish by her actions. They all let him alone, and he was very grateful to my mother.

Castle Garden, New York, was the dumping ground for all kinds of cargo, and it was also crowded with emigrants. The floor was greasy and dirty. Here we had to make our beds on the floor, as did all the other emigrants. Mother spread out the quilts and bedding, and we all lay down in a row, the children and Mother and Father. There were sacks of brown sugar at our heads. My little brother was sleeping next to me, and in the night he awoke and whispered, "Alma, there is a hole in the corner of this sack, and I am going to have some of the brown sugar." We had not had any sugar or candy all the way over, so we got a spoon out of the box and had all the brown sugar we could eat. In the morning we were so sick! We did not care for brown sugar after that.

We traveled by train to Omaha, Nebraska, where we started on our long journey with eighty wagons in our train, under the direction of Captain Murdock.

One night we traveled all night long. The Indians were so bad; they had stolen a woman from a train ahead of us, so we walked all through the night to escape them and get past their camps. This night it was very difficult for my father to keep up with the wagon train. He kept going slower and slower because of his rheumatism. I kept hold of his hand and tried to help him as much as I could. Finally he could not keep up with the train any longer, and told me to keep hold of the last wagon and continue on and he would catch up with us later when we camped. He was finally left behind. Soldiers were camping in the hills and had a big bonfire. Father mistook this for our camp and went in that direction. When he got there, he was surprised to see so many soldiers. He did not know how they would accept him. They asked him what he could do, and he said he could play the violin, so they had him play all night long.

In the morning, one of the men brought him to our camp just as we started out to travel on. Mother had cried all night because she was afraid the Indians had taken him and she would never see him again. We all thanked our Father in Heaven that he was with us again, for the train would have had to start on without him. It was too dangerous to wait for anyone.

After three and one-half months walking over a hot desert, up the rugged hills, and down the hills and canyons, we finally came out of Emigration Canyon, dirty and ragged. When I saw my mother looking over this valley with the tears streaming down her pale cheeks, she made this remark: "Is this Zion, and are we at the end of this long, weary journey?" Of course to me as a child, this had been a delightful pleasure jaunt, and I remember it only as fun. We children would run along as happy as could be. My older sisters used to make rag dolls as they walked along for us little children to play with. But to my mother, this long, hot journey with all of us ragged and footsore at the end and the arrival in the valley of desert and sagebrush must have been a heartbreaking contrast to the beautiful home she had left in Sweden. But to me and to my mother, the gospel had been worth all it had cost.

ȣ

Alma Elizabeth Mineer's family lived temporarily in Mount Pleasant and Brigham City, Utah, before settling in Salt Lake City. While a teenager, she became an exquisite seamstress, making fine dresses for the wealthy women of the valley and costumes for the Salt Lake Theater. She was a cast member for many productions in the theater. Alma Elizabeth married Joseph Henry Felt in 1875 at the age of twenty, and they became the parents of six children. They adopted four additional children. She died July 29, 1950, in Salt Lake City, at the age of ninety-five.

Source: Alma Elizabeth Mineer Felt. Journal. In *An Enduring Legacy,* 7:193–232.

MARGARET GAY JUDD (CLAWSON)

Born: September 6, 1831, North Crosby, Leeds, Canada
Parents: Thomas Alfred and Teresa Hastings Judd
1849: Allen Taylor Company
Age at time of journey: 17

Our journey was like all such journeys—it had its pleasant side, and its unpleasant side. When the sun was shining and the roads were good, we trotted along feeling that we would soon be at our destination, but when the rain poured down and the roads were so bad that we could not travel—then that was the other side.

While moving from New York to Nauvoo, Illinois, another man and his family traveled with us. His name was Chauncey Noble. A better, pleasanter, and more agreeable man never lived, but his wife was just the opposite—always grumbling, fault-finding, and wanting to go back. She never would camp out with the rest of us. Her husband always had to get a bed for her at some farmhouse along the way. How often it happens that good, kind men get vixens for wives, and amiable women get brutes for husbands. So it is, and always will be.

What a pleasant trip it all was for us children. Nothing to worry us; that part of it was all left for our parents. Oh, why can't children appreciate the happy, careless life they have before coming to the years of responsibility! Trifling things make deep impression on children's minds. I remember today a sight I witnessed on our journey. After traveling all day, we camped just before sundown in a nice place, not far from a farmhouse. When Mother commenced to get supper, she gave me a little tin pail and told me to run across the way for some water. When I got to the well-curb, there was a man sitting close to it and looking right at me. He had no eyelids, no nose, nor lips. Well, it didn't take me long to get back to Mother, without any water either but almost scared to death. If Mother had not gone for the water herself, she never would have believed that I had good reason to be frightened. He certainly was an awful sight. Those staring eyes! Those grinning teeth! That noseless face! He haunted me for nights. Father afterwards learned that this poor man had had an accident, while making potash, that burned his flesh off.

On the road to Nauvoo, we passed through Kirtland, Ohio, and camped not far from the temple, and we were given permission to go through it. I well remember with what awe we entered it. My parents looked very serious and spoke quite low and cautioned us children not to speak at all. The impression remains with me today.

In the fall we came to a little place in Illinois called Walnut Grove. The greatest recollection I have of Walnut Grove is of the big watermelons and the great amount of black walnuts that grew there. Riley (my brother) and I went one day with Father and gathered up a heaping wagon load of them. We put them in the garret of the log house we then lived in and feasted on them all that winter.

The next move we made was to a little town called La Harpe, twenty-five miles from Nauvoo. Father was anxious to get a good stock of provisions before going to Nauvoo, as they were very scarce and high there. Mother would have gone right on without a loaf of bread, she was so anxious to be where she could see and hear the Prophet Joseph Smith.

Father planted us a garden that spring. The vegetables grew very fast, but the weeds grew faster, and Mother made Riley and me do the weeding (or some of it). We used to say if it were only shady and we could sit down, it wouldn't be so hard, but to go right out in the hot sun and stoop over to pull the weeds—we thought it awfully cruel of Mother to have us to do it. She often used to show us how to do it. It seemed so easy for her. Why, she could pull more weeds in five minutes than we could in half an hour, and still she insisted on us doing it. Oh, the hardships of childhood!

After the Saints left Nauvoo, my parents redoubled their exertions to get an outfit to go to the Rocky Mountains. How well I remember what a hard time Father had breaking in the animals to draw the wagon. There were six cows and two oxen. The oxen were well broken and quite sedate, but the cows were wild and unruly. Father would get help to yoke them up and then would start to drive them. All at once they would run off in an opposite direction from where he wanted them to go or would run around to the back of the wagon and get all tangled up. This went on for days and days, and while Father was breaking the cattle, Mother was praying. She afterwards told me that many nights when we were in bed asleep, she would go out into the orchard at the back of our house and there pour out her soul in prayer, asking the Lord to open the way for us to go with the Saints. She was willing to share their privations for the sake of being with them.

After weeks of hard work, Father had the cows broken so that he could drive them, and on the ninth day of May, 1849—my brother Riley's sixteenth birthday—we said good-bye to our friends and relatives, got into our wagon, and started on our long, eventful journey. Oh, how Mother's countenance beamed with joy! What did she care for hardships, if she could only reach the goal?

One of many little romances: The night before we left, my true lover, Henry Ridgley, came to bid me farewell, and under our trysting tree (a big tree close by) we each vowed eternal constancy, for four years at least. At the end of that time he would be of age, and then he would come to claim me for his own, even if I was at the end of the earth. Well, he did come to see me, but it was forty years after instead of four years. He had a wife and three children. I had a husband and was the mother of thirteen children. The romance of youth gone, the reality here. How we did talk of the long ago and laugh at each other's inconstancy. After a pleasant two weeks' visit with us, he returned to Springfield, and in five years after, I received a letter from his wife telling me of his death.

We camped in Council Bluffs, Iowa, for one month waiting for companies to be made up. Oh the monotony of camp life when not traveling! How delighted we all were when we started on our journey for good. Everything was bright and beautiful. I was young and healthy. All was "color de rose" for me. The responsibilities, anxieties, and cares rested on my parents.

There were several nice young men in our company, which made it interesting for the girls.

On the fourth of July we camped for the day, not entirely to celebrate but to wash and do mending and various other things that were necessary. We camped in a pretty place near a creek. I was to wash with my sister Phebe's help. She was only twelve but very energetic. We selected a place, quite secluded, close to the creek where we could have plenty of water. Well, we were making suds when a dapper young gentleman from New York, a nephew of our captain, who was on his way to California, discovered us and brought a large piece of delicious fruit cake, which was made to celebrate the Fourth on the plains—it was a rather embarrassing position to accept this compliment in the midst of soiled linen and soap suds, and I had not been introduced to him before. However, I accepted the cake with great patriotism, and from that time he often called at our wagon, that is, our wagon yard. So when any of the young folks called, I was as much at home sitting on an ox yoke as if I were sitting in an easy chair in a parlor. Such is life on the plains.

There were several very nice young men in our company. Especially one. He used to say such lovely things to me—told me that I was beautiful and intelligent, and even went so far as to say that I was amiable, something I had never been accused of before. He told me that I was the only woman he ever loved and that we were just suited to each other. I began to believe him, and when he proposed, what could I say but "yes." Well, the course of true love did run smooth, at least until we got into the Valley. Then we had the usual lovers' quarrel but not the usual making up. In a short time he let me know that another girl appreciated him, if I did not. He married one of the girls of our company, whose ignorance he had ridiculed to me many times while on our journey. Such is the constancy of man! I understood she made him a good wife but stood in great awe of him, the man who had honored her so highly. The fates seem sometime to interfere with our plans, all for our best good.

My brother drove an ox team across the plains for a widow and her little girl. The little girl was very sweet and amiable, the mother rather peculiar. He said that the girl would ask more questions in a day than ten men could answer in a week. He was a born joker and could no more help joking than he could help breathing. He could never tell her anything so absurd or ridiculous but what she believed it. He got so tired of her questions, such as "Riley, I wonder how far we have traveled today, and I wonder how far we will travel tomorrow," "I wonder if we will get to water," "I wonder if we will see Indians, and I wonder what they will do," "Will they be friendly or savage?"

The "wondering" got so monotonous Riley could hardly stand it. At last he had his revenge, when we came in sight of Chimney Rock, Nebraska. (Anybody who has crossed the plains either by wagon or rail will remember seeing this landmark.) It is very tall and shaped something like a smokestack and probably centuries old. At the rate we traveled, it could be seen several days before we reached it. The girl began her speculations about the rock, and he told her in a most confidential way that as soon as we got to it, he was going to push it down, that he was sick and tired of hearing so much about Chimney Rock, and that it had stood there long enough anyway. As soon as he got his hands on it, over it would go. Well, she begged and implored him to let it stand, that other emigrants might see it who came after us, but he was obdurate. She then threatened to tell "Brother Brigham" when she got to the Valley. That was always her last resort. He kept her anxiety at fever heat for two days until we were within about a half mile of it. He then gave in to her pleadings and said he would let it stand. She was so delighted that she gave him an extra good dinner and supper that day.

One cow in our team was very intelligent; in fact, she was so bright that she used to hide in the willows to keep from being yoked up, but when father found her and yoked her, she was a good worker and a good milker. She got very lame at one time and could scarcely travel. My parents were very much worried, having already lost one cow. They were afraid they could not keep up with the company, and so Mother said she would make a poultice and put it on as soon as Bossy lay down for the night. Mother made a very large plaster that covered all the cow's lame hip. Well, the next morning when Father went to get the cows up, he called out, "Why, Mother, you have poulticed the wrong hip." Mother said, "Never mind; it's all right, it has gone clean through;" and sure enough, Bossy limped a very little that day and was soon as well as ever. I know there was a great deal of faith mixed up with that poultice.

Along in the early fall, we used to find wild fruit, such as chokecherries, service berries, and a little red berry called buffalo or squaw berries. One day I decided to have a reception that evening, so after we camped, I asked some of the girls and boys to come and spend the evening at our campfire after their chores were done. Verbal invitations and short notice never gave offense then. All were delighted to come, no regrets. In the meantime, I had asked Mother to let me make some buffalo berry pies. Of course she did. Pies were a great luxury and were seldom seen on the plains. I wanted to surprise my guests with the sumptuousness of my refreshments, and I did. Well, I had hardly got the ox yokes and some other things artistically arranged before my company arrived. After we had chatted awhile and sung songs together, I excused myself to go into the pantry (a box under the wagon) and brought out my pies. In passing the pies, I rather apologetically remarked that they might not be quite sweet enough. One gallant young man spoke up very quickly saying, "Oh, anything would be sweet made by those hands." And I believed him. After serving the company, I joined them with my piece of pie. Well, with the first mouthful—oh, my, how it set my teeth on edge, and tasted as if it had been sweetened with citric acid! That ended my pie making on the plains. I often wondered how my friends could have eaten it, but etiquette demanded it. I don't think there was enough sugar in the camp to have sweetened that pie.

At last we came to the end of our long, tedious journey, and on the evening of October 15, 1849, we camped at the mouth of Emigration Canyon. Oh, what a glorious sight it was to look down the valley of the Great Salt Lake!

The next morning we were up bright and early and soon drove down. In the meantime, Brother and Sister George Stringham, old friends and neighbors in Springfield, who came to the Valley the year before, sent word to my parents to come to dinner and to camp on their lot. Never was an invitation more gladly accepted.

That dinner—can I ever forget it?—never before nor since have I tasted anything like it. There was a nice, juicy, fat beef pot roast, baked squash, boiled potatoes, mashed turnips, and boiled cabbage. It seemed very extravagant to have so many kinds of vegetables, but Sister Stringham wanted to give us a real treat, knowing that we had not eaten any kinds of vegetables since leaving home. Everything tasted as if it had been sweetened with sugar. It was a feast fit for the gods. I wonder how our fancy cooks nowadays would like to get a full dinner in an open fireplace with wood for fuel and very few cooking utensils. That was the way we got our meals in those early days.

∽

Margaret Gay Judd married Hiram Bradley Clawson, a close associate of Brigham Young, in 1852. They became the parents of thirteen children, including two sets of twins. Margaret was known for her keen sense of humor, her poise and charm, and her devotion to her family. She spent the later years of her life working in the Salt Lake Temple. She died February 10, 1912, at the age of eighty. Her son Rudger Judd Clawson was called as a member of the Quorum of the Twelve Apostles in 1898. He was president of the Quorum from March 17, 1921, until his death, in 1943.

SOURCES: Margaret Gay Judd Clawson. Reminiscences, holograph. LDS Church Archives. Manuscript is also filed in the Library of Congress in Washington, D.C.

See also "Reminiscences of Margaret Clawson." *Relief Society Magazine* 6 (1919): 251–62, 317–27, 391–400, 474–79, 505–9.

Mary Ann Stearns (Winters)

Born: April 6, 1833, Bethel, Oxford, Maine
Parents: Nathan and Mary Ann Frost Stearns
1852: Harmon Cutler Company
Age at time of journey: 19

Parley P. Pratt married Mary Ann Frost Stearns, a widow, when her daughter Mary Ann was four. When this account opens, Elder Pratt was on a mission to South America.

With the close of January, 1852, leaving Kanesville, Iowa, all dances, festivities and amusements ceased, and our hearts and labors were turned to the preparation for our journey to the valleys of the Great Salt Lake. We had no idea how we were going to make the journey, but all were told to get ready, with the promise that the Lord would help when they had done the best for themselves that they could. I think our hopes must have been greater than our faith, for there was not the least chance in sight for us to make the journey. What we needed was a wagon, team, provisions to last three months, and a driver, and where they were to come from was a mystery to us.

One bright Monday morning in the early days of May, A. W. Babbitt called at our door and said to my mother, "Sister Pratt, I am just starting for the Valley. I have put a hundred dollars in the emigration fund with the express purpose that you have a good substantial comfortable wagon to make the journey in across the plains, and I want you to be sure that you get it." She thanked him for his thoughtfulness in our behalf, and he was off on his long journey westward. We looked at each other in astonishment, Mother and I, for his promised help and blessing had seemed to drop right down from heaven in our behalf.

Two days later, Joseph A. Kelting called to say good-bye, as he was going back east to Philadelphia to visit his old home and to buy goods for his store and would not cross the plains for another year or so. He said to Mother, "Sister Pratt, I have put one hundred dollars in the emigration fund with the express understanding that you have a suitable and comfortable outfit for the long and tiresome journey that lies between us and your friends in the Salt Lake Valley. It is there for your benefit, and I want you to have it."

Words failed to express our gratitude for the help offered in our time of great need. We had been living by faith, and now the substance was growing large in our sight, and we marveled at the providence of our Heavenly Father in our favor.

Mother proposed that we take our sewing and visit Mrs. Ellison for an hour or two and bring some butter home with us. After the greetings were over, Sister Ellison began to inquire about our prospects for the journey, and Mother told her we had the promise of a wagon and thought we would have plenty of provisions to last us, but we did not know where a team and driver were coming from. Sister Ellison turned from her work and raised her hand, saying, "Well, I can tell you about that right now. There is a brother boarding with me who has been working all winter to get his team, and he wants to go in someone's wagon and drive this team. He will furnish his own provisions and would desire to have his washing done in return for his services. He will be up to supper at six o'clock, and you must stay and see him, for I believe it is just the right chance for both of you." All of these opportunities had come to us in a short space of about one week.

As our ox team was to be our companion on the journey, perhaps it will not be out of place to introduce them by name. Dick and Darby were their names when they were purchased. Brother Murie, our driver, called the cows Lady Blackie, Lady Milky, and Cherry. And the one that was the most vicious, he said, was Lady Lucifer, since it was the most proper name for her.

We made a nice camp one night, pitched the tent which Brother Murie and James had all to themselves, and we retired with the prospect of a good night's rest, but in the night a thunderstorm arose. It rained and lightninged and blew a small hurricane, and as the storm increased, Mother proposed that we should be ready for any emergency. Our wagon stood broadside to the wind, and with every fresh gust it seemed as if the bows would snap in spite of us. We tried to hold against the wind, but our strength was puny. Brother Murie had taken the same precautions that we had, was up and dressed and holding on to the tent to keep it to its fastenings. Jimmie, covered up in bed, was still asleep, as were the children in the wagon. As the ground was sandy, some of the pins pulled loose, and the tent collapsed and buried them in its wet folds. This aroused Jimmie, and he scrambled around but could not find his clothes, and it was with difficulty that they could get out from under the heavy, wet tent. Mother handed out a big shawl to wrap Jimmie in, and they climbed into the wagon, and with our united efforts we pressed against the bows until the storm subsided. Mother fixed a place on the foot of the bed for Jimmie and covered him with some extra bedding, and the rest of us sat and nodded until daylight, thankful that the Lord had preserved us from the destroying powers of the elements. The sun came out warm and smiling as if nothing had ever happened to disturb our peace.

We could now knit or sew comfortably, as the teams were jogging along the level ground, and I made us some heavy white shirts to use when the cool weather should come and knit some cotton stockings to wear as we were going along. We had a new wooden tub, and we would put some cold water in it in the morning and set our butter and other things in it, cover it thickly, and it answered quite a good purpose as a refrigerator—not making the butter exactly ice cold, but better than melted butter. Our morning's milk we put in our new tea kettle, placed a cloth under the cover, put a cork in the spout, tied a cloth over that, and tied it to the reach under the wagon; and no matter how hot the day was, the draft under the wagon made it very comfortable for our dinner, for there was a piece of butter the size of a teaspoon bowl, which was very fresh and sweet, and the children took turns having it on bread.

There was one thing that we enjoyed very much, and that was the bath in the river. The men of the camp found a convenient place down the river and had their swim in the daytime. We could always tell when they did this, because they came into camp looking so fresh and clean, for most of the time they were a dusty lot. And the sisters each procured a bathing suit of some kind, and we took our baths by starlight. We were afraid to go far from the shore on account of the quicksands. We would make a line from the nearest to the shore and the farthest ones out could get a good ducking without much danger. We were very still about it all, for we never could tell when Indians might be lurking around, and we slipped into our beds quietly, greatly refreshed and thankful for the opportunity.

One night there came up a big windstorm, not rain, but a dry, hard wind, and it seemed to me that it blew harder and harder with every gust. Our wagon was just a few feet from the bank, and it was twenty feet down to the water, and I was on the side next to the river. And, oh, how I did suffer with fear that night. I thought I could feel the wagon tipping many times. Mother tried to comfort me, telling me of the many times the Lord had brought us through trying scenes in the past and that His hand was still over us to protect and save. About daylight the wind began to abate, and by sunrise it was a calm, still day again, and we traveled on as usual.

After camping the night of August 16, 1852, at Deer Creek, Wyoming, the travelers made needed repairs on their wagons, did washing, and prepared for the Sabbath, the following day. The next morning they held a worship service in a small grove that included seats, a rude platform, and a pulpit erected by a previous company.

That familiar hymn "How Firm a Foundation" was sung, and after a prayer by one of the aged brethren and another hymn, testimonies were borne, and counsel and instruction given by the captain. And all felt to renew their diligence in serving the Lord, and with fresh hope in their hearts to soon meet with the faithful in the Valley. After the close of the meeting and the noon luncheon had been partaken of, they enjoyed a season of quiet rest till the lowering sun admonished them to prepare for the night. And just as the evening meal was about ready, a carriage was espied coming from the East. Some going out to meet it, word was soon sent back that it was Apostle Lorenzo Snow just returning from his mission to Italy. He camped with us that night. The people met and received instructions and counsel from him for their future guidance and encouragement, and he told them of some of his experiences on his mission.

And now an event occurred which changed the current of life for me.

The "event" to which Mary Ann was probably referring was her marriage that very evening, August 16, 1852, to the teamster Oscar Winters, a member of her company. Sadly, Mary Ann ended her account without giving any information about the wedding. A note appended to her account tells us that the ceremony was performed by Apostle Lorenzo Snow. Their wedding meal was bread baked on a skillet, a piece of meat, and a little lump of fresh butter, with a cup of cold water. The note also adds this information: "She [Mary Ann Winters] laments even in the long years after her marriage date that she had no looking glass, and this was a trial as the hair must be arranged smoothly, every hair in place, as she was anxious to please her young husband. But it was great fun, she says, using Oscar's money after reaching the Valley, to buy things at Kincaid's store, trembling a little inwardly lest the clerk should discover what a new housekeeper she was."

❧

Mary Ann and Oscar Winters arrived safely in Utah and settled in Pleasant Grove. They had eight children. Their daughter Augusta became the wife of Heber J. Grant, seventh President of The Church of Jesus Christ of Latter-day Saints. Mary Ann died April 2, 1912, in Salt Lake City, Utah.

SOURCE: Mary Ann Stearns Winters. In *Treasures of Pioneer History*, 1:473–85.

Part Eight
TEENAGE DRIVERS

"Let your light so shine before men, that they may see your good works, and glorify your Father which is in heaven."

꩜ MATTHEW 5:16

President Brigham Young knew that teenagers enjoy driving. Beginning in 1860, President Young tried a new way to transport immigrants across the plains. He decided to send "out and back" wagon trains—"out" from Utah to Florence, Nebraska, to pick up merchandise, machinery, and immigrant baggage, and then "back" to Utah. (They were also known as "down and back" trains.) Needing drivers for the Utah wagons, he called many young men in Utah on "out and back" missions during the spring and summer. Between 1860 and 1869, most immigrants arrived in Utah walking beside one of the Church wagon trains.

These wagon trains did not leave Salt Lake City empty. They were stuffed to their bows and covers with flour, tents, and other supplies, which were dropped off at various stops on the way east for use on the return trip.

At the eastern end of the journey, these young men were virtual taxi drivers, taking wagons into Florence, Nebraska, picking up passengers, and shuttling them to various campgrounds, where final preparations were made for the long journey. In addition to their responsibilities as teamsters, these Utah boys gathered firewood, built fires, tracked down missing cattle, helped set up and break camps, and spent hours in rivers helping wagons to cross. They repaired harnesses, shod horses and oxen, fished, swam, and filled their hats with berries.

By the time the "out and back" riders were active, the trail was a virtual highway of activity. One teamster recorded in his diary that on one day in 1861 he met 205 emigrant teams bound for California. Two weeks later he passed a large band of Sioux Indians on their way to fight the Pawnees. Large numbers of overland travelers in search of gold, furs, or adventure passed or were passed by the trains of the Latter-day Saints.

The "out and back" drivers were not the only young teamsters. Many wagons in the regular pioneer companies were driven by adolescent boys and girls. It was not uncommon to see girls as young as eleven holding the reins of frisky, hard-to-manage teams of horses. Eight- and ten-year-old boys and girls walked alongside yokes of oxen, urging and prodding them along the seemingly endless trail. They were a remarkable group of young people, these teenage teamsters, who contributed in an important way to moving Zion westward.

RACHEL EMMA WOOLLEY (SIMMONS)

Born: August 7, 1836, Columbia County, Ohio
Parents: Edwin Dilworth and Mary Wickersham Woolley
1848: Brigham Young Company
Age at time of journey: 11

How long it was after the Prophet Joseph Smith was killed before the Saints began to leave Nauvoo, I cannot say, but previous to our leaving I became acquainted with two old Scottish ladies by the name of Sutherland. They had never been married and consequently hadn't had any children. They always made much of me, as I was a favorite of theirs and loved these old ladies with all my heart. There was not a day passed but what I spent some portion of it with them. Many a nice apple or bit of cake they have saved for me, and when the Saints were leaving Nauvoo, they were afraid they would be left. I begged Father to take them with us, but he couldn't as he had all that he could do to move his own family, but I was not satisfied, for I did not want them left behind. So I went to Brother Edward Hunter, who is bishop of the Church. He lived opposite us and had plenty of money then as now. I was very intimate with his family, or his wife, I might say, for that was all the family he had at that time. So, as I have said, I made bold to ask him to rig up a wagon for the old ladies. I pleaded with all my heart. I remember he had at that time an old dump cart, and I asked him if he was going to use it, and he said no. I told him that it would do for them, and they would be so glad to have even that good. I said one yoke of oxen would be enough to take them. When I said all I could say, and he listened with great patience, he patted me on the head and said, "There, there, you are a good little girl to think of them. I will see what I can do for them." But I had to go and leave them after all. I never knew whether they were brought out of Nauvoo or whether they suffered with other Saints that were left behind.

There are a few instances I remember of our journey to Winter Quarters. I remember recrossing the Mississippi with Father a few days after we left, and in that short time the mob had destroyed many of the houses. Ours was in an awful state. The doors were off the hinges, the windows broken, and the well almost filled up with rubbish.

We left Winter Quarters the first part of May, 1848. We traveled a few miles the first day and camped on what was called Horn, or Elk Horn, River. We had three wagons and a light spring wagon for Mother to ride in, as her health was rather delicate at that time. [She was expecting a baby.] Her wagon was fixed very comfortably, so she could have her bed made all the time, and she could lie down if she wished. My brother Frank was to drive a wagon, but he had to drive Mother, as one of our teamsters left soon after we started, so then I had to drive. I did so in fear and trembling, as one of the horses was very vicious. She used to kick up dreadful until she would kick the board of the wagon all to pieces, but it made no difference, I had to go at it the next day just the same.

When we got fairly started on our journey, there was a very large company; I think there were two hundred wagons traveling up the Platte River. The wagons were divided into sections. President Young headed one section. That was a dreary part of the journey. For miles and miles, one could see nothing but the unbroken plains. Not a tree or a shrub in sight, nothing but the white dusty road as far as the eye could see. At night when the camp was reached, myself and companions would always make a rush for the river to bathe. It was great enjoyment after the warm, dusty day.

While traveling, there was always someone sent ahead on horseback to search out the best place for a camp; then when it was reached, the wagons at the head of each line would stop, and the next one would drive just as close as possible to it, then the next, and so on until they were all in each row formed into a semicircle, with an opening at the beginning and end. These gates or openings were left so the animals could be driven out and in. There was a guard placed both in the corral and out, and I often think of the cheery call of the guard when all was quiet in camp. It was in this wise, "Twelve o'clock in the corral, and all is well." Then the next would take up the call, until each one of the guards had given the hour.

July the fifth we were camped on a small stream called Goose Creek, in Wyoming. It was here that my sister Mary Louise was born. We never laid over a day in consequence of Mother's sickness. The Lord blessed her and fitted her to bear the journey, as he did many others at that time. I have heard her say she never got along better in her life. Mary grew so fast she was one of the finest of Mother's children, even if she was born under difficulties. We had to burn buffalo chips while coming up the Platte. I used to get out just before camping, take a sack, and fill it as our journey progressed. When we got into the Black Hills, our companies were divided into tens, so they were called, because the facilities for camping were not so good for so many in one place.

We heard so much of Independence Rock, in Wyoming, long before we got there. We nooned at this place, but Father stayed long enough for us children to go all over it. I went with the boys and with Catherine. It is an immense rock with holes and crevices where the water is dripping cool and sparkling. We saw a great many names of persons that had been cut in the rock, but we were so disappointed in not having a dance. Our company was so small, and we had not a note of music or a musician. We camped that night on the Sweetwater River. The companies ahead of us lost a great many animals at this place due to the minerals in the water. The stench was awful, and the wolves were as thick as sheep. It seemed as though they had gathered for miles around. There wasn't a wink of sleep that night for any of us. The wolves were so bold they would come right into camp, and some of them would put their feet on the wagon tongues and sniff in at the end of the wagon. This was my birthday; I was twelve years old.

Another day I was driving as usual, and to make matters worse, we had an old pig that was expecting babies that day, and she had to ride in the buggy, as Father was very anxious to save the little pigs, but they all died in consequence of the rough road. I remember I was so glad when we camped that night, because I was so completely tired out with the road and the frisky horse.

I don't remember anything else of note until we drew near our journey's end. We came to what is called Big Mountain, in Utah, and it is rightly named. We had to double teams to get up, that is, take all the teams in camp and put them all on two or three wagons, take them up to the top, then go back for others. Then coming down, we had to put them on the back of the wagons to hold them back. Those that came when we did know something of the difficulties of traveling. Five months of that kind get monotonous after a while, but we were so near our journey's end that we could rejoice even withall.

Coming down the mountain, the axle tree on Mother's wagon broke, which caused some delay. Father cut a young tree and fastened it under the wagon so that it could be brought into the Valley.

With what gladness we got our first glimpse of the Salt Lake Valley. We camped just at the mouth of Emigration Canyon in the afternoon to wash and fix up a little before meeting our friends that had preceded us the year previous. Uncle John had been here a year and was living in the Fort, as it was called. His wife had supper ready—corn, cucumbers, and other vegetables. I have no doubt but what we did justice to that supper, being the first in a house for five months. We went to Brother Ensign's, who kindly offered us the hospitality of their one room until we could do better. So we pitched our tent in his yard and settled down to rest after our long journey. We arrived September 22, 1848.

∽

Rachel Emma Woolley married Joseph Marcellus Simmons, a Church public works bookkeeper, in the Great Salt Lake Valley at the age of fifteen. The marriage ceremony was performed by President Brigham Young. Rachel became the mother of ten children. Her sister Mary, who was born on the plains, became the mother of J. Reuben Clark, who served as counselor in the First Presidency to three Presidents of the Church. Rachel Simmons was left a widow at age thirty-five. She became a practicing midwife at age thirty-eight to support her large family. One of the babies she delivered as a midwife was Spencer W. Kimball, who became the twelfth President of The Church of Jesus Christ of Latter-day Saints. She died November 30, 1926, in Salt Lake City, Utah.

SOURCES: "Journal of Rachel Emma Woolley Simmons." In *Heart Throbs of the West,* 11:161–63.

See also Leonard J. Arrington and Susan Arrington Madsen, *Sunbonnet Sisters, True Stories of Mormon Women and Frontier Life,* 40–45. Salt Lake City: Bookcraft, 1984.

EBENEZER FARNES

Born: February 4, 1843, Dagenham, Essex, England
Parents: John Burnside and Ann Isacke Farnes
1862: Benjamin Hampton Freight Train
"Out-and-back" teamster
Age at time of journey: 19

At about nineteen years old, in April, 1862, I emigrated for America, on the ship *William Tapscott*, with 852 passengers. This ship was a three-mast sailing vessel, old and worn out, an old tub not fit for merchandise but good enough to carry "Mormons" on.

About the third week on the voyage there came a terrible storm, which tore everything down that could be broken. So bad was the storm that the people had to stay in their beds for three days, the hatchway being closed most of the time, the water being one foot on the first and second decks, washing from one end of the ship to the other and side to side as the ship tossed and rolled. The Captain said it was the worst storm he had ever seen, and he had been a captain for twenty-five years. The ship sprung a leak, and the pumps had to be kept going night and day until we reached New York. When the Captain was asked about the storm, he said if he had known the condition of the ship he would not have sailed on her but consoled himself that, as he had a load of "Mormons" on board, he would get through all right, as there had never been a ship lost that was carrying Mormons. After the ship landed in New York, she was not considered fit to carry anything back but lumber, so they loaded her with that, and she got waterlogged and was lost at sea.

Taking the voyage all in all, it was quite an experience for us all. There were only two deaths, one child and a man who was sick when he came on board. The burial at sea is a sad thing. The body is sewn in a canvas, and a ball of iron placed at their feet so as to make the body sink feet first so the sharks cannot get it. A long plank is placed on the rail of the ship, part on the ship and part over the water, and the body is placed on the plank, feet to the water. After the burial ceremony the plank is lifted at one end, and the body slides into the sea. You can see the body go slanting down for a long distance.

During the calm, the emigrants had a good time playing on deck, climbing up the riggings, dancing, and playing games. One game we played all the time was pumping water out of the vessel, about ten men at a time on the pump. One of them would sing all the time, making up the song as he pumped. But it helped to break the monotony. I remember on one of the calm days the ship lay in the water rolling from side to side, and the porpoise, a fish from four to six feet in length and as fat as a pig, was playing about the ship, and the water [was] like a sheet of glass.

Ebenezer crossed the plains with a freight train, where he was employed as a cook. For his work he was paid $35 for the entire trip.

We made pretty good time on the plains, but it became monotonous day after day, the same old thing—we get up in the morning at 4:00, make a fire, cook breakfast, eat, and get ready to start at 6:00 or 7:00 A.M. It was hard on me, as I had a very bad leg through a kick one of the boys gave me because I beat him in a wrestling match. My leg got so bad that my shin bone was bare for four or five inches and made me very lame, but I got along as well as I could riding in the wagon, sometimes on good roads, until we reached Green River. The river was very high that year, and it was very dangerous to cross it. However, the captain found a gravel bar so that we could cross the stream. We started to cross when the third team got stalled in the river, and my leg hurt me so much standing in the water up to my waist that I started to pass the team that was stuck. The captain saw me and came dashing up to me and commanded me to stop, for if I had gone twenty feet further across the stream, my team, wagon and myself would have gone down the river and perhaps been lost, as the bar in the river was narrow, and there was not room for two teams to pass each other.

I had to stand in the ice cold water for more than an hour. At first my leg hurt me, then got numb; at last it seemed no use to me. I had to drag it along like a piece of lead, but at last we got across the river and camped. After turning our cattle out to feed, I got back to the river and took my boot off, and the sight of my poor leg made me feel sick. The flesh of my leg around the sore place looked all white, like a piece of boiled tripe. I wrapped up my leg and thought perhaps I could get to Utah and then have it taken off. Pleasant thoughts for a young man all alone in the desert. But from that day forth the sore did not pain me so much, and day by day the wound got smaller and smaller, so when we got to Salt Lake City, the wound was more than half closed and soon got well.

After arriving in Utah, Ebenezer made arrangements to work supplying the Church blacksmith shop with charcoal. In return, the Church agreed to bring his parents and the rest of his siblings from England to Nebraska. From there, the Church would bring them to Utah through the Perpetual Emigrating Fund. Ebenezer walked eighty miles round-trip to a post office in Utah to mail his

family in England a letter telling them they could now come to Salt Lake City.
He writes of meeting them on the plains.

In the fall of 1863, I was asked at a minute's notice if I would take a pony team and go back on the plains alone and meet all of the companies and ask them if they would need any tents and transact other business. I told them I was ready to start that day, so they started me off without any provisions or cook. I took twelve tents, some oats for the horses, some flour and some bacon. I tried to buy some bread but could not get it. I traveled about forty miles a day, rather lonesome, but then I should see my father, mother and my sisters on the way.

About noon I met two men on horseback. I asked them how far Captain Daniel McArthur's train was behind, and they told me about three miles. I asked if a family named Farnes was in the train, to which they replied, "Yes, your father died yesterday," and rode on. The blunt way in which he told me was almost more than I could stand. The contrast between my feelings before and after he answered me is too great to imagine. The joy I hoped to experience upon meeting my father and mother and loved ones soon was dispelled by the knowledge that my father died the night I camped at South Pass, Wyoming. It broke me down. I stopped my team and could go no further, as I felt my heart would break at meeting the train. I lay beside the road, weeping tears from my heart, if there is such a thing.

After a while the train came in sight, and they passed me, but I could not muster courage enough to meet my mother. After a time I drew myself together, knowing that they would camp soon. I hitched up my team and turned back and overtook the company just as they were making camp. I found the wagon they were in and after a while went there and found my mother in a burning fever—the mountain fever—we call it typhoid fever. My mother did not know me. She thought it was my brother M. H. and called me her Matthew. My sister Matilda, age eighteen, was just getting over the fever, while the others, Jane, my sister, age fourteen, John Lyons, an adopted brother, age three, and Mary Ann French, a British emigrant who would later marry my brother Matthew, were worn out with sickness and the death of Father. Father had walked from early morning until 11:00 P.M., and while putting up a tent for the girls, fell down three times and was dead in less than an hour. He died at 12:00 P.M. and was buried at daylight with the dead sweat all over his body, and all this hurry because Captain Andrew McArthur of St. George, Utah, wanted to make a record of making the best time and by bringing his cattle in the best shape across the plains.

After staying at the camp until the ox teams were ready to continue the journey, I bid good-bye to my mother. It was hard for me to turn my back on them and go three hundred miles east. A young man volunteered to go back with me and show me the way where my father was buried. My intentions were to dig up the grave and see if he was dead when they buried him, as one of the men who helped to put him away told me he did not think Father was dead, as his shoulders were warm with sweat.

The next day I saw one of the sights of the desert. Near the crossing of the Sweetwater River, there had been a large number of cattle die at one time from minerals in the water, and they were lying in the center of the road. We saw seventy-five or eighty of the large prairie wolves eating the carcasses that lay there, and about one hundred coyotes standing nearby waiting until the wolves were satisfied. These wolves were the largest kind, and there were enough of them to have eaten us both and my team in less than an hour. I did not feel much afraid of them as they had plenty to eat, and they will only attack a man when they are hungry or wounded.

Well, it was a sight to see their long hair and bushy tails shining in the sun, their red mouths open, and their white teeth snarling at us as we passed through, some of them not more than twenty-five feet from our team. It was quite a relief when we got past them and out of sight. Few men have seen such a large number of grey wolves at one time.

That evening we got to the place where my father was buried. The grave was all that one could ask for, under the circumstances. After a few hours' rest we journeyed east and soon met another emigrant train.

This company was under Captain William Hyde. After being with this company an hour, a sister came up to me and asked me to go to a poor Welsh woman and try to get her to take something to eat, as she had not been out of the wagon for two days. She and her husband had been quarreling two days before and she was sulky. I went to the wagon and spoke to the woman but received no answer. I looked closer and could see part of her legs, her body being covered. I put my hand on her and asked her to get up, as there was a brother from Salt Lake City who wanted to talk to her, and again received no answer. I told her if she did not get out I would pull her out by the feet. No answer came, so I started to pull her by the ankle and found she was dead.

∾

Ebenezer Farnes married Mary Catherine Bullock and Veta Josephine Fjeldsted. Mary had five children, and Veta had nine. He spent most of his life in Logan, Utah, where he was a butcher. He died February 13, 1920. His grandson was Harold Silver, an important inventor of agricultural and mining machinery used throughout the world.

SOURCES: Ebenezer Farnes. Reminiscences, typescript. LDS Church Archives.

See also *The Story of Ann Isacke Farnes and Her Family,* compiled by Marilyn Austin Smith and Glenna King Austin. Typescript, 1972, in possession of family.

ZEBULON WILLIAM JACOBS

Born: January 2, 1842, Nauvoo, Hancock, Illinois
Parents: Henry Bailey and Zina Diantha Huntington Jacobs
1861: Joseph W. Young Wagon Train
"Out-and-back" teamster
Age at time of journey: 19

Zebulon Jacobs crossed the plains for the first time in 1848 at the age of six. In 1861, when he was nineteen, he was living in Salt Lake City. President Brigham Young asked him to return to Nebraska to help transport immigrants across the plains. Zebulon drove one of the forty wagons that rolled out of Salt Lake City around April 23, 1861. Three other trains left too, totalling two hundred wagons that headed east that week.

May 19. Left camp 8 A.M. Made seven miles to Devil's Gate, in Wyoming. Dug out a piano and several sacks of salt that had been cached four years ago by earlier pioneers. They were not damaged in the least.

July 1. We had three blankets and one buffalo robe for three of us to sleep upon. Woke up in the morning feeling rather cold. Felt for blankets, and blankets were gone. Looked and saw William Biler some six or eight feet away on one side and Samuel L. Sprague about the same distance on the other with a blanket each. I had possession of the robe.

July 4. It being the glorious day of which every true American is proud, we tried to be as jolly and happy as possible. In the morning we had an Indian War dance in costume. In the afternoon a sham battle between Indians and white men, which was well done. Towards evening we had a grand circus, which pleased the people very much. Our Indian exercises frightened some of the new drivers very much till they were made acquainted with the program.

July 23. Went eight miles in the morning and drove nine miles in the afternoon. Camped. Wood rather scarce. Had to watch the mules pretty close to keep them out of the corn, being camped close to some fields.

July 24. It being the anniversary of the landing of the pioneers in Great Salt Lake Valley, we were up at daylight and called out the National Guard, the teamsters, who fired a volley of musketry and any other kind of guns that were handy. Then the martial band struck up "Hail Columbia" (the band being composed of tin pails, pans, kettle lids, bells, and various other instruments of music); then there was another volley by the Guard. At sunrise, the firing of cannon (which was about three inches in length). We concluded the morning performance with an Indian jig. In the morning went eight miles, in the afternoon went nine miles, at sunset the firing of a cannon. In the evening we had a grand ball at (what our tent was called) the Bachelors Hall.

July 31. Out early. Helped shoe an ox. Looked and saw that the mosquitoes and horseflies were driving off the horses and cattle; had to keep what is called the dog trot for about a mile before I caught up with them. Caught a horse and jumped on and with considerable difficulty I got them back to camp.

August 2. I fixed the mules' feet, mended harnesses, and played laundress. In the evening I went to meeting, but the mosquitoes were there first. The mosquitoes sang at the opening, sang during service, and at the closing, and finally sang all night. Tried to sleep, but they pulled me out of bed.

August 4. Went to the river to have a bath. We found mosquitoes there too. They very soon got rid of us. I then went to a meeting. The meeting was well attended. Mosquitoes came in clouds. The people soon went in disgust to their tents but not to sleep. No, no, that was impossible.

August 16. This morning a mule took the rope that I was leading it with and landed me after various gymnastics about twenty feet distant from the place that I had ought to have occupied. Hurt my foot a little. It is very disagreeable traveling, on account of the softness of the soil and a number of spring streams that cross the road. I came very close to stepping on a rattlesnake. Considerably scared. Killed it and went to camp.

August 17. As we woke up in the morning, all hands that were in the tent began laughing at each other's faces. We came to find out we all had our faces besmeared with tar and wagon grease. Some of the boys from the other camp had paid us a visit and left their compliments upon our faces. Helped shoe several oxen. Received several pretty severe raps from the oxen floundering.

August 24. Henry Parker and myself went on guard. About 10 P.M. we saw a man coming towards us. We hailed him and found that he belonged to Heber C. Kimball's train, which was a short distance ahead. The Utah boys had got him to catch rabbits in Yankee fashion by building a small fire and lying down by it with an open sack for the rabbits to run into, and then hitting them on the head with a club, now and then giving a low whistle, the other boys going out to drive the rabbits in.

All of a sudden the boys gave a yell. The man thought that the Indians were upon him, and off he started at full run. He had run about a mile when we stopped him. The fellow was scared out of his wits. The cause was that he knew everything but Yankee tricks. We took him back to his train, which was three-fourths of a mile distant. The method of catching rabbits just described was a trick.

❧

Zebulon Jacobs made "out and back" trips again in 1862 and 1863. He married Frances Woods Carrington, and they became the parents of five children. He served in the

Blackhawk War as a sergeant in the cavalry. He became a railroad man, working as a conductor on the Utah Central Railroad. Later in life he became a guard at the Utah State Penitentiary. Zebulon died September 22, 1914, in Salt Lake City. His mother, Zina D. H. Young, plural wife of Brigham Young, became the third general president of the Relief Society, serving from 1888 to 1901.

SOURCES: Zebulon Jacobs. Reminiscences and Diaries, holograph. LDS Church Archives.

See also William Hartley, "Diary of a Teenage Driver." *New Era,* July 1984, 8–11.

LIST OF PHOTOGRAPHS AND ILLUSTRATIONS

List of Photographs and Illustrations

Edwin Alfred Pettit, page 71. Photograph from Rebecca Nelson.

George Sudbury Humpherys, page 74. George Sudbury Humpherys (seated in middle) with his brothers and sisters (left to right): Hyrum, Thomas, Sarah Jane, John James, Harriett, and Samuel. Photograph from Kathleen Bergsjo.

Fanny Fry Simons, page 76. Photograph from Georgia G. Hansen.

Part Five: Suffer the Children, page 81. Wagons at Coalville, Utah, ca. 1867–68. Photograph from LDS Church Archives.

Mary Ann Weston Maughan, page 85. Taken from a portrait found in the Daughters of the Utah Pioneers Cache Museum, Logan, Utah.

Christian Lyngaa Christensen, page 88. Age: early thirties. Photograph from Joseph C. Christensen.

Mary Goble Pay, page 91. Photograph from Marjorie Hinckley.

Susan Noble Grant, page 96. Susan Noble Grant seated in center. Women beside her are unidentified. Photograph from LDS Church Archives.

Part Six: Life on the Plains, page 103. Wagon train, ca. 1868, Echo Canyon. Photograph from LDS Church Archives.

Sarah Sophia Moulding (Gledhill), page 107. Photograph from MarLaine Layton.

Mary Jane Mount Tanner, page 111. Photograph from University of Utah, Marriott Library, Special Collections.

Willam Henry Freshwater, page 114. W. H. Freshwater Store, once a popular gathering place for the men of Provo, ca. 1923. William Freshwater is standing in front of door. Others in photograph are unidentified. Photograph from Wanda Kirkwood.

Lucina Mecham Boren, page 117. With Lucina Boren are her grandchildren Wilford Boren and Tella Boren Gardner. Photograph from Daughters of the Utah Pioneers Museum, Salt Lake City, Utah.

Catherine Adams Pilling, page 121. Age: approximately sixty-five. Photograph from E. Harris Adams.

Margaret McNeil Ballard, page 124. Margaret McNeil Ballard and her twins, ca. 1868. Photograph from Janet G. Ralph.

Lucy Marie Canfield Margetts, page 128. Photograph from Julia Carver.

Part Seven: Fun and Romance, page 133. Council Bluff's Ferry. Engraving by Charlles B. Hall, New York. Photograph from LDS Church Archives.

List of Photographs and Illustrations

Alma Elizabeth Mineer Felt, page 137. George Albert Smith (left) and David O. McKay (standing right), with Alma Elizabeth Mineer Felt (seated center) and Calleen Robinson (seated right), Days of '47 Queen, 1947. Photograph from LDS Church Archives.

Margaret Gay Judd Clawson, page 141. Photograph from Daughters of the Utah Pioneers Museum, Salt Lake City.

Mary Ann Stearns Winters, page 148. Photograph from Daughters of the Utah Pioneers Museum, Salt Lake City.

Part Eight: Teenage Drivers, page 153. Wagons crossing the Platte River. C. R. Savage, Photographer. Photograph from LDS Church Archives.

Rachel Emma Woolley Simmons, page 157. Photograph from LDS Church Archives.

Ebenezer Farnes, page 162. Photograph from LDS Church Archives.

Zebulon William Jacobs, page 168. Photograph from Oa Jacobs Cannon.

General References

Arrington, Leonard J. *Brigham Young: American Moses.* New York: Alfred A. Knopf, 1985.

Bitton, Davis. *Guide to Mormon Diaries and Autobiographies.* Provo: Brigham Young University Press, 1977.

Ellsworth, S. George. "The Mormon Trail." In *Pioneer Trails West,* edited by Donald Emmet Worcester, 166–83. Victor, Montana: Western Writers of America, 1985.

Kimball, Stanley B. *Heber C. Kimball: Mormon Patriarch and Pioneer.* Urbana: University of Illinois Press, 1981.

Kimball, Stanley B. "Historic Resource Study: Mormon Pioneer National Historic Trail." United States Department of the Interior/National Park Service, Washington, D.C., 1991.

Knight, Hal, and Stanley B. Kimball. *111 Days to Zion.* Salt Lake City: Deseret Press, 1978.

West, Elliott. *Growing Up with the Country: Childhood on the Far Western Frontier.* Albuquerque: University of New Mexico Press, 1989.

INDEX

Index